PENGUIN BOOKS

The AFTERLIFE CONFESSIONAL

Bill Edgar is the one they call the 'Coffin Confessor' – he's a successful businessman, counsellor, author and one of Australia's leading private detectives, who's known for doing what most lawyers, accountants and professionals won't, can't or fear: speaking the truth of those silenced.

ALSO BY BILL EDGAR

The Coffin Confessor

Last Call for Tell-All

MORE TRUE STORIES FROM THE COFFIN CONFESSOR
BILL EDGAR

PENGUIN BOOKS

PENGUIN BOOKS

UK | USA | Canada | Ireland | Australia
India | New Zealand | South Africa | China

Penguin Books is part of the Penguin Random House group of companies whose addresses can be found at global.penguinrandomhouse.com

First published by Penguin Books, 2024

Copyright © Bill Edgar, 2024

The moral right of the author has been asserted.

All rights reserved. No part of this publication may be reproduced, published, performed in public or communicated to the public in any form or by any means without prior written permission from Penguin Random House Australia Pty Ltd or its authorised licensees.

Pseudonyms have been used in this book and other details altered where necessary to protect the identity and privacy of people mentioned.

Cover design and image by Alex Ross Creative © Penguin Random House Australia Pty Ltd
Author photo © Justine Walpole
Typeset in Minion Pro by Midland Typesetters, Australia

Printed and bound in Australia by Griffin Press, an accredited ISO AS/NZ 14001 Environmental Management Systems printer.

 A catalogue record for this book is available from the National Library of Australia

ISBN 978 1 76134 325 4

penguin.com.au

We at Penguin Random House Australia acknowledge that Aboriginal and Torres Strait Islander peoples are the first storytellers and Traditional Custodians of the land on which we live and work. We honour Aboriginal and Torres Strait Islander peoples' continuous connection to Country, waters, skies and communities. We celebrate Aboriginal and Torres Strait Islander stories, traditions and living cultures; and we pay our respects to Elders past and present.

This book is dedicated to the man I was looking for but could never find until I saw him in my reflection

Contents

1	Another man's grave	1
2	Going global	13
3	Paid in full	39
4	Material girl	59
5	Ash traveller	79
6	Till death do us part	105
7	Back on the horse	131
8	The confessional	153
9	Worse than death	175
10	Die living	205
	Acknowledgements	225

1

Another man's grave

Let's start my story where most people end theirs, lying in a grave.

Flat on my back, I looked up and could see the colours change where the gravedigger had busted through the various layers of soil. At the bottom it was rocky and lifeless, followed by lighter dirt packed less tightly, right up to the rich topsoil. At the very top, eight feet above me, I could see the odd blade of grass peeking over the edge. It framed a blue sky with clouds scudding across my window to the world.

It was a hot and windy day but the soil beneath my back was actually pretty comfortable. Damp but not wet, cool against the oppressive heat. *Not bad*, I thought to myself. *I could get used to this.*

But let's rewind a bit.

My name is Bill Edgar. Better known these days by my professional title, the Coffin Confessor. Among other things, I crash funerals and deliver eulogies on behalf of the deceased. It's a job that I sort of fell into. One I never expected to have. Mainly because it didn't exist before I started doing it.

How I got into it is a long story. I won't go into too much detail here because I've already written a book about it – which you might have already bought and read – and I don't charge my clients twice for one service. I've got a code. A flat fee. Fair price. No refunds. I haven't been asked for one yet.

It all started when I told a dying man, Graham, that I'd crash his funeral for him. Graham had vultures in his family and a toxic best mate who was trying to get it on with his missus. There was nobody who would tell the truth of Graham's life after his death, and he joked that I may as well be the one to do it. That joke grew into a plan – to actually crash his funeral and deliver his preferred eulogy. I attended as one of the mourners, sat among his family and friends, and at the designated time when his so-called best mate was doing the official eulogy, I stood up. 'Sit down, shut up, or fuck off,' I began. 'The man in the coffin has something to say. And this is it. "You know, friend of mine, you've been trying to screw my wife while I'm on my deathbed. I couldn't get up. I couldn't yell. I couldn't kick. I couldn't scream. I couldn't defend my wife or my family. But I found someone who could . . ."'

And that was that. A reporter heard about the incident, wrote a story about me that went viral, and then all sorts of media started approaching.

The job has grown a lot since then. I don't even know how you'd describe what I do now. I guess it's an all-inclusive service fulfilling people's last wishes. A concierge service for those who are desperate and dying and need one final request to make their passage a little more special. I'm a bit like the bloke in the lobby of a fancy hotel who knows how to open doors and make things happen in a strange city – but I do it for people checking out for good who have a final piece of baggage they need handled.

The baggage is as unique as the people who engage my services. Sometimes I'm spilling a long-held secret. Other times I'm visiting the homes the dying have left behind to destroy evidence and make sure their secrets stay that way. Sometimes it's taking revenge on someone who's wronged them, or seeking forgiveness from those they've wronged.

No two requests are the same. But there are similarities. We all leave this world with similar regrets. As some cunt whose name escapes me once said, 'Ashes to ashes, dust to dust.' Buried, burned, whatever happens to us, we all end up in the ground eventually. Most people die with baggage from mistakes they made. Or mistakes they *wish* they'd made. Regrets about what people didn't do are just as common as regrets about what they did do. Many, many people check out of this brief-stay hotel wishing they'd sampled more widely from the buffet.

Ancient cultures believed that life's two motivating forces were sex and death. They weren't wrong. A good proportion of people I've helped had fucked up their lives through sex. Falling in love with the wrong person. Or too many at once. I'd also include money on that 'motivating forces' list. Throw in religion. Family too. Sometimes a combo of both of those things. The old one-two punch of being on the outer of a religious family is going to have you on the ropes from an early age. A lot of funerals I've crashed have been for people who've abandoned their churches. Or, more accurately, who've been abandoned by them.

So I've heard it all. Final requests that have made people cry their guts out. Or chuck their guts up. Terrible, terrifying, perverted things. I don't mind. Keeping an open mind is a good trait for anyone to have; for me it's a professional necessity.

Confessing your deepest darkest secrets isn't for everybody, but we all die with at least one big one. Most take it to the grave. Some think it's not worth it to confess. Others believe leaving a shit storm behind will only hurt those they love. Even more have been wronged so badly by the people who were supposed to have loved them that they die without ever speaking up. For all of them it's easier to avoid confrontation and let the innocent go meekly to the grave.

But this just allows the guilty to remain free.

I've never been backwards in coming forwards. I always speak my mind and confront those who wrong me. That's not for everyone; most people don't want that sort of aggro. It's not that I seek it out, but when it comes knocking, I'll gladly open the door.

So I'm happy to lend a hand. As I say, I'm not afraid of confrontation. Thrive on it, in fact. What started very early as a defence mechanism against childhood dangers has become something I've used my whole professional life – as a fighter, then a private investigator, and now as the Coffin Confessor. More and more, I've found myself fulfilling the role of someone who helps people confront their demons while they die. How that happens has changed a fair bit in the past few years. And every case is different.

* * *

In early 2021 I received a call from a gentleman named Max. Max was in desperate need of assistance and was willing to pay top dollar for it. Paying the fee wasn't the problem. Ironically, having too much money was. They say money is the root of all evil; it was certainly the start and end of Max's particular problem.

Max was an old-school, company-town kinda guy. He'd lived and worked in Wollongong on the New South Wales South Coast his entire life, beginning his career with the steel giant BHP in the age of both the resource boom and hefty union pay packets. Safe to say, he'd done very well for himself. He was in his late seventies, retired and living in a nursing home by the time I met him. The home was paid for with a fraction of his wealth. The question of what would happen to the rest of it was why he hired me. Personally, I thought he was seeking a way of buying more time, but time is the one commodity that can't be bought.

Max was dying. He was out of time and out of sorts with his family, who were scheming by his deathbed. It's no secret that there are vultures in families. Almost every family on the planet has at least one member who will see the death of a loved one as a free-money buffet. In Max's case he was surrounded by them, and they were eagerly rubbing their hands together, hoping to get the last of the old man's riches. Two sons, a brother and an ex-mistress had their eyes on what Max would leave behind. After all, like the saying goes, you can't take it with you. Or could he?

Max asked me to visit a shipping container storage facility not far from where he once lived. While the hovering vultures knew Max had stuff in storage, they didn't know *exactly* what he had stashed away and they couldn't get into the facility until he passed. Nor did they know what intel the other family members had. They could only guess and stare each other down while they circled his deathbed in ever smaller circles.

The facility was accessed using a passcode. Once through the security-coded gate you needed a key to open the actual container. I had both and set up a camera to record myself entering and recovering Max's property. The container was full of antique-style furniture and boxes of odds and ends from a time long gone. I left that for the vultures. On Max's instructions I was there to collect a box – no larger than your average shoebox – that contained cash, jewellery, two gold bars and a number of documents he wanted kept private. Max had given me a mud map of sorts that helped me locate the box among the antiques and the dust.

Just as I grabbed it, a man walked past the container, did a double take, and took a few steps back. 'Hi, my name's Stephen. Did Max pass away?'

'Max is still with us,' I answered carefully. 'But he's entrusted me to collect and deliver this box to him.'

Stephen nodded and explained that he was the manager of the complex. He knew no one could get into the container without a key and a passcode. As such, he was sure I wasn't a thief and knew I must have been hired by Max. As Stephen left he asked me to pass on my best wishes to the old man.

I did as requested the next day as I sat by Max's bedside and showed him the video I took of me entering the container and removing the shoebox. As was my standard procedure, I also recorded the contents of the box so he knew exactly what was there. Max showed little interest. He knew what was in the box, his only concern was what was going to happen to it.

He told me to burn the cash and bury the rest of the items somewhere no one would ever find them. That first request was a problem. Burning cash is technically illegal in Australia. While my work means I have a 'complicated' relationship with the police and generally walk a very fine legal tightrope, I try not to fall onto the wrong side if I can help it. For every parasite attached to a family, there's an even more blood-sucking lawyer attached to them. There's usually a small army with a grudge against me, and sure as shit the minute I cross the line one of them would be all over me. There's nothing parasitic types would like more than seeing me fail, so I tread very fucking carefully indeed.

I explained all this to Max, and how I couldn't destroy the money as he'd asked. But I could bury it alongside the other valuables, someplace that not even his greediest relatives would think to look.

He was delighted and his face lit up like a kid seeing a Christmas tree for the first time. 'They said I couldn't take it with me,' he said with a huge grin. 'This'll show them.' Max couldn't stop smiling as we discussed the plan, but he still had concerns. 'How can we trust the funeral director? Won't he just steal it? Or the gravedigger?'

'Everyone has a price,' I said. 'Even gravediggers.'

I was happy to take a cut out of the fee Max was paying me to pay off whoever I needed to. A dying man had entrusted me to carry out his last wishes and I was paid handsomely to do so. I viewed the cash, jewellery and gold he wanted to disappear as less valuable than the satisfaction he'd get in knowing his family of vultures would never lay eyes on any of it. Let alone their hands.

With that, we sealed the deal. I took my leave and, in time, Max took his.

* * *

Max was buried just outside of Wollongong on a hot and windy Thursday afternoon. His funeral was attended by just nine people. Fortunately, one of those nine was Max's trusted confidant. He'd agreed to keep me informed of Max's passing and time of burial.

The grave had already been dug when I arrived. The mound of dirt beside it was covered with fake grass until the time came to fill the grave in. A gazebo was set up to provide shade, along with some plastic chairs for the comfort of the mourners. I'd already spoken with Cliff, the man in charge of digging and filling in the graves. I was up-front – I told him about Max's wishes to be buried with some personal items. I was vague about exactly what those items were, and Cliff didn't really want to know, but he did have some questions. 'Why don't you just put them in the coffin with the body?'

'Max is worried the funeral director might take them out,' I explained. I offered Cliff $200 for his time, effort and discretion. He gratefully accepted.

Armed with a small spade and the shoebox, I asked Cliff to lower me into Max's grave. I climbed onto the backhoe he used for digging through the rock and was lowered down. Once I reached the bottom, Cliff pulled the backhoe up to give me room to move. As I stood there an overwhelming feeling of loss and loneliness hit me. I'd never felt anything like it, not as a street kid sleeping rough, not even when I was in solitary confinement in jail.

Another long story for another time, but in brief, when I was seventeen, I spent some time incarcerated in Brisbane's infamous Boggo Road Gaol. Boggo Road was a place you learned to pack away your fear. You weren't going to survive very long if you let fear in. Boggo Road was brutal, even by the standards of Aussie prisons. It scared the guards just as much as it did the inmates. The whole place stank of fear. The halls, the walls, the cells and even the iron bars all told a story of horrific abuse and trauma.

My stay was short compared to some, but harsh all the same. I was basically a boy when I went in. A big boy physically, but a scared little kid inside, already badly traumatised by years of sexual abuse. And Boggo Road was crawling with predators. I made sure my back was always to the wall and I never let my guard down. I soon discovered that the nicest-seeming prisoners were often the most depraved.

When I was first confronted by a fellow inmate for sex, a real aggressive mental case, I wasn't sure whether to run, hide, fight, or curl up into the foetal position. But instinct, previous abuse and the streets had all taught me that most people have a front and if you get past that front you expose their weakness.

With one blow from my elbow to his chin the creep hit the ground. 'Listen, bitch,' I snarled, looming over him, 'you're lucky I don't put a shiv in your spine. Stay the *fuck* away from me.'

The words were barely out of my mouth when I was dragged away. The guards booked me for fighting and tossed me in my cell without food or water for two days. Two very long days and nights, while my mind worked like a shovel, turning the same thoughts over and over. *What if he dies? What if his head hit the concrete when he fell and that makes me a murderer? Even if he lives, what if he presses charges? I'll be stuck in here for years, maybe even decades. Fuck, Bill, what have you done?*

The guy lived and eventually they let me out, but the scared kid who went into that cell never really left. He's still there, freaking out, in fear of the predators who wish him harm, and of the harm he could do to others. Those two days in the slot was the last time I felt so helpless or let myself fear for my own safety. Fear was not an option. You could enjoy all sorts of luxuries in Boggo Road – drugs, moonshine, violence – but fear wasn't one of them. I learned to keep it out of mind. The problem is, when you bury one feeling in order to survive, you end up burying the lot.

So I wasn't expecting to feel fear, standing in the dirt on a hot Thursday afternoon back in 2021. I hadn't felt so helpless since I was a boy and I had to get out of there. But first I had a job to do. I started to dig as hard and as fast as I could, but every time I thought I'd dug deep enough, Max's shoebox seemed to have grown. I kept digging and digging, and trying to jam the shoebox into the hole I was creating at the bottom of the grave, but it was no good. Just as I finally got the hole deep enough to fit the shoebox snugly, I heard Cliff yell out, 'I'll be back in a minute!'

'No worries!'

Bullshit. I had plenty of worries. While those words shouldn't worry anyone, try hearing them standing in a grave knowing that the only person who knows where you are and is your only way out is fucking off for who knows how long.

* * *

You know that saying about being buried 'six feet under'? I can tell you that's bullshit too. I'm six foot one and I can assure you I was standing at least eight feet below ground. But what can you do? Out of options, I finished burying Max's shoebox and waited for Cliff to return.

I never thought I'd be there. I hate spending time in a graveyard when I'm not on the clock. And I don't want a funeral. I don't want to be buried in a fucking hole in a cemetery run by a bunch of pricks who tell people what they can and can't do when someone's paying their respects or leaving flowers or mementos. I'm going to be cremated and thrown in the ocean followed by a bottle of port. Afterwards, my nearest and dearest will have a dinner to celebrate my life. While this will last for just a moment, the memory of me will live on in those I truly touched. That's what matters to me in life, so that's what I want from death. Not this burial bullshit.

I had time to think while I was at the bottom of that grave and I decided to do what I never thought I'd do. I had a little rest. The walls were compacted soil and the base of the grave was smooth enough. There were no worms or bugs. No signs of life at all, actually. So I lay down and looked up at clouds scudding across that blue sky. I took a few pictures and thought how this would soon be Max's final resting place, his neighbourhood for the rest of time. Once the panic and fear passed, a weird feeling of acceptance came over me. In some ways being left in a grave was inspirational.

It might sound morbid, but I envy the dead. Not because they're free of pain or suffering but because they know what I don't. Not that I want to know just yet. I did know that my nearest neighbour was lying about two feet away. In fact, I had neighbours on all sides. To be honest, I didn't want to meet any of them. I've had enough cunts of neighbours topside; I didn't want any disputes down here. But I understood how a lot of people think death is a transformative experience. I'm not sure if I was letting something go or taking something on. Probably both. A fair trade, Coffin Confessor style.

Lying in another person's grave even for a few minutes got me thinking about my own life, death and everything in between. What I took away is that I hadn't changed my mind about my plans. I'm not going to be buried. The grave wasn't all that bad but give me the ocean over the dirt any day. More importantly, I decided to find more time to reflect on where I am, never forgetting where I came from. Life isn't just about moving forward. It's about living and doing everything to the best of my ability while knowing that without pain and hardship I wouldn't be who I am today.

While life seems to be travelling at a speed I can hardly keep up with, I have a habit of stepping to one side and just watching the world pass me by. I've become accustomed to watching and observing. I can tell the seasons are changing by the way in which the trees on my property change colour; the number of birds in the sky; snakes sunbaking in the grass or baby animals calling out for their parents.

When I die, life won't stop for the rest of you; you'll continue to eat, sleep and drink, go to work, laugh and cry. You'll continue to live your lives the best you can. When it's your time the same will happen for those you leave behind. It's a never-ending cycle of life and death, death and life.

2

Going global

Recently, I've had to face an elephant in the room. It's something I never anticipated when I agreed to crash my first funeral. The elephant is I've become something of a celebrity. Believe me, it wasn't my doing or my intention. I got a media profile quite by accident. But hey, it is what it is.

It began not long after my first couple of crashed funerals. Reporters started calling and requesting interviews. I wasn't sure if it was a good idea to expose myself to public scrutiny, especially since I was a private detective whose livelihood depended on discretion and keeping a low profile. But the more I thought about it and talked it over with my wife, Lara, the surer I became that what I was doing wasn't illegal, immoral, or to the detriment of the dead and dying. I was offering my voice to those who couldn't speak. Not just my voice but my arrogance and attitude too. I've got aggro to spare for those so-called loved ones lingering by the deathbed of a relative or friend in the hope that they'll be named in the will. It's those vultures and fake friends that allow me to crash funerals without caring what they think of me. I don't give a fuck about them. My compassion and duty of care are reserved for my clients. And that's what I wanted to put on the record when I agreed to speak to the media.

I was inundated with requests for interviews but agreed to just one, with a reporter not far from where I live near the Gold Coast. To my surprise, that one interview went global. It became clear that one story wasn't going to be enough, and soon I had journalists from all over the world wanting to know more. I had no choice but to step in front of the camera and tell the world about the Coffin Confessor. And to be honest, I quite liked it.

I wasn't sure what the public would make of my crashing funerals, though. Part of me was expecting people to react with disgust or horror, but I was surprised to find that most people seemed to like what I was doing. Or if they didn't like it, they understood. Sure, there were some who thought it disrespectful or distasteful, but I was taken aback by how understanding and interested people were.

When the reporters started calling, I chose to look on the sunny side. Suddenly, I was doing media all over the world. I went from PI work, discreetly camping outside cheap motels to photograph cheating blokes stepping out on their wives (let's face it, if men kept their dicks for their partners and people were true to their vows, PIs would be out of a job), to fielding calls from Hollywood producers who wanted to buy the film rights to my story.

For a while, I was doing two to three media appearances a day. In the morning, I'd be on Australian radio, at lunchtime I'd be on national TV in South Africa, then I'd record an interview for a podcast out of the US. It went nuts, which is kinda cool. I figured every media appearance was free advertising and would get the word out to the people who needed my services. So I always said yes.

I thought I'd embrace it by getting custom COFNFSR number plates on my favourite car. If that sounds like it's in bad taste, then remember who I am and what I do – and the service I was advertising. Why not boast about it on my ride? For the record, it's a 1974 Ford XB Coupe. For readers who aren't into muscle cars, the XB Coupe is similar to the one that Mad Max drove around Australia after the apocalypse. It's a beautiful car, one you can hear coming from miles away – but that of course was an issue. The car loudly announced I'd arrived at the client's funeral – giving those the deceased wanted confronted a chance to fuck off before proceedings began. It made my job a little bit easier on one hand, and a little harder on the other. The biggest downside was that mourners were now focusing on me, rather than their dearly departed.

* * *

In the early days, I thought I'd try out an idea for a side business while I had everyone's attention. People from all around the world were reaching out wanting to meet the Coffin Confessor. For the most part, they were people who didn't want to hire me. Some got in contact just because they wanted to meet me. They looked to me for some kind of wisdom or perspective on the fact they were going to die. That, or they wanted a shocking, controversial experience they could tell their friends about. So I thought, *Why not kill two birds with one stone?*

THE AFTERLIFE CONFESSIONAL

I decided to explore a concept that's as controversial as crashing funerals but a lot more hands-on: Coffin Camping. A chance for people to come and stay on my property, meet the Coffin Confessor, and get an up-close-and-personal look at their own mortality by experiencing a night in a coffin. The concept gripped the media as much as anyone else. But it was over almost as soon as it began.

I designed a campsite on my property, a lovely bit of land on the edge of the rainforest on Tamborine Mountain near the Gold Coast. I trucked in three shipping containers – one converted into a recreational room with a lounge and bar, the other two converted into tomb-like bedrooms, each with two coffins set up for a bit of eternal slumber. At least for one night. The idea was to provide something like a sensory deprivation float tank. Encourage people to spend a night contemplating death and exploring their inner self – and have a fun, cathartic experience at the same time.

After a couple of months' research and development I was ready for business. I listed the unique concept on Airbnb and was immediately inundated with requests. Mostly from journalists! They all wanted to try before they die and I was happy to oblige. To be honest, I didn't expect it to be so popular. I thought I'd get one or two curious punters – maybe some goth kids on their honeymoon.

Before it ended, I did meet some rather intriguing people. Many campers came just to meet the Coffin Confessor and confess all sorts of fucked-up family secrets they felt they could share with me.

Speaking of fucked up – Coffin Camping quickly became that. It was a good idea in theory, but in practice it was a nuisance.

People kept trespassing on my property, taking photos, driving past and screaming things out the window. Some would even pull up to the gate and yell requests for their burial. 'Bury me in satin! Pour one out on my grave!' That was annoying. After just two weeks someone offered to buy the whole concept. So I closed up shop. Coffin Camping came and went faster than a fat kid falls off a seesaw.

I wasn't unhappy to see the back of it. The way it played out, I couldn't get through a day without some tourist rocking up to my property and wanting something from me. And I already had a lot on my plate.

*　*　*

Being a minor celebrity must be an uneasy feeling for some but the only time I feel uncomfortable is when I'm invited to the local RSL for dinner, or I have to visit a client in hospital. That's because when I show up, the implication is clear – someone doesn't have long to live. Lately, whenever I walk into a hospital, I can feel the eyes of the patients and staff following me around. I once heard someone mutter under their breath, 'Look out, here comes the grim reaper.' I try not to make eye contact with the staff, but I make sure that every elderly and sick person I pass receives a warm smile. I hope it gives them comfort and conveys that I'm not there for them, and that I'm more the *grin* reaper than the grim reaper.

Another downside of having a profile is that it's now harder to do my job. When people start whipping their heads around and whispering when I arrive at a funeral service, it creates a certain anticipation that I'm about to do something crazy. Sure, I might be, but the fact that people are concentrating on me rather than on remembering the deceased isn't what the client signed on for. I get that crashing a funeral is a semi-public spectacle, but it's also a private one.

When the Coffin Confessor is engaged, it's a strictly confidential arrangement until death. No one other than the client, the Confessor and maybe one other trusted individual knows the confession and the details of what is to be done or said. Discretion out of respect for the dying is paramount.

Ideally, when I arrive, I get mistaken for one of those nameless faces you always see at funerals – a one-time work colleague maybe, or a neighbour who's just come to pay his respects. I'm usually very discreet and am pretty good at blending in. I speak only to those who speak to me. For the most part, I observe the crowd, watching for that one toxic mourner who's likely to cause a scene once I start causing mine. I can always spot them. The one family member who shouldn't be there, or a friend who might have wronged the deceased and is lurking with a sour look on their face. Locating them is a necessary precaution before crashing a funeral. If I'm trying to get a read on the assembled mourners, and they are able to ID me first and cause trouble, then the whole thing risks going down the drain.

In the normal course of things, if all goes well, I'll slip into the chapel or gravesite and sit among family and friends. I usually do this without speaking to anyone, or maybe just offering simple condolences in return if they're offered to me. Then, at the specific time as directed by my client, I stand up and interrupt the service. I read aloud my client's confession, quietly place the written confession on the coffin, and leave. I have no idea if the funeral is going to continue or not. When it's my time to shine, it's over as quickly as it began. By the time the mourners have gotten over the shock, I'm halfway out the door. I never stay for the wake and mingle over drinks, finger food and conversation. Once I'm done, I'm done. My client is dead and I've delivered their confession and carried out their final wish. I'm paid to vanish as quickly as I appear – and I get paid very well to do that. After all, as I explain to new clients at the start of our relationship, they don't need the money where they're going. And I've never had a complaint.

* * *

While I don't get complaints, I do go out of my way to make sure that my clients can trust me to take the greatest duty of care. Take Marcus, for example.

Marcus had a sense of humour. He was an Irish immigrant who'd arrived in Australia in the early 1980s and settled down in the northern suburbs of Melbourne. He'd heard about the Coffin Confessor via a true crime podcast and was so intrigued he decided to make contact. He had a very funny request. In every sense of the word. While he wasn't afraid of dying, a quirk of family history had given him a strangely specific fear.

Marcus's grandmother passed away in Ireland, and during her funeral, it was discovered that her body was not in the coffin. There was someone there, but it was an elderly gentleman. Not an easy mistake to make, you would think. You'd actually be amazed at the negligent stuff that can happen in funeral homes. Like my own industry – it's very difficult to lodge a complaint from the grave. It's the Wild West out there.

Just recently, a funeral home in Colorado in the US was raided because neighbours reported a terrible smell. Investigators went in, did their thing, and found 189 decaying bodies on the premises. It wasn't a serial killer's morbid hoard – just a terminally dodgy funeral company not doing their job. For whatever reason, the bodies hadn't been burned, and fake cremation papers had been filed. Worse, the families were given *some* ashes, which might have in retrospect been concrete powder disguised as human remains. So a bunch of American families who thought they were scattering Grandma on the shore of a lake were actually flinging around cement while her body was rotting away in some coolroom. That's an extreme case. Thankfully, it's not common for the wrong body to be at the wrong funeral, but shit happens.

Anyway, Marcus was adamant nothing like that was going to happen to him, and wanted someone to check halfway through the funeral that they were burying the right corpse. In his final days, he wondered who he could trust. Who did he even know that had the balls to open a coffin midway through a service and double-check the right order had come out of the kitchen.

He thought about asking a family member or a good mate, but didn't want a loved one to have the image of him dead in a box in their memory banks forever. Plus, he didn't want there to be a fight between family and friends. Then he heard about me and the light bulb went off, and so he engaged the Coffin Confessor. Easy enough.

His only other request was that I make a bit of a joke of the whole thing and have the musical theme to 'Pop Goes the Weasel' playing as I walked through the church and opened the casket lid. For no particular reason, other than he thought that was the funniest possible song to play at a funeral. Easy enough. I could play it on my phone, but I wanted to make sure I was up to the task of opening a coffin during the service. That's easier said than done. Not all coffins are the same design – some have hinges, some are sealed in place by careful grooves in the wood. That's before you even consider hidden locks, secret openings, and so on. Coffins are often hard to open unless you have a key or a screwdriver – or you know the manufacturer's tricks.

I had to know what type of coffin my client was going to be in. I'd look like a complete fucking idiot struggling to open a box with 'Pop Goes the Weasel' playing in the background. What was I supposed to do if the song ended and I was still trying to get the lid off? Start the song again? Ask the funeral director if they could help? No chance; I had to prepare and find out the type of coffin my client was going to be cremated in and take it for a test drive.

This turned out to be more involved than I'd imagined. Some manufacturers don't want you to know their secrets and dismiss your questions, while others will gladly answer them. The reason most funeral homes are reluctant to spill their secrets is because of the markup. They buy the coffins at a certain price, then add their own significant amount on top of that. Most if not all manufacturers refuse to sell directly to the public or risk upsetting their biggest customers, the funeral directors. Just another one of those annoying backhanded deals between businesses. This one was particularly rude because who is going to shop around and negotiate on price when they're grieving a loved one? A good rule of thumb – the higher the stakes, the bigger the graft. It's human nature for people to want to know the secrets of others while at the same time hoping theirs will be kept safe from prying eyes and ears. But I'm very good at finding out secrets.

I decided to visit a number of funeral homes. The directors, thinking they had a sale on their hands, were happy to oblige. I was shown a wide variety of options. High-end and mid-range coffins, as well as coffins that resembled layers of cardboard crudely glued together. All the same basic idea, but they all had their own little quirks, and I needed to know as much as I could about each one. More importantly, I needed to know how to open them quickly and without issue.

By the day of Marcus's funeral, I was probably the world's greatest expert on breaking into a coffin. In prison I once met a man who could hot-wire any kind of car he came across. He knew every trick in the book to get them up and running. I felt a little like him, but with arguably a less universally useful skill to have in the back pocket.

Turns out I didn't need to do all that homework. When I arrived at the service, Marcus was lying in a coffin I was already familiar with. Someone very dear to me was once buried in the exact same box. The only difference was this one had been customised with personalised graphics of Marcus's greatest loves – his two German Shepherd dogs. I'd also made contingencies. As I scanned the hall, which resembled a small indoor theatre, I counted a total of nine people including the funeral worker I'd had a quiet word with before the ceremony. I'd already arranged for him to leave the coffin unlocked – in return for a little spending cash.

The one thing about people is that they can always be bought. While some will deny this, most quickly change their tune if you show them enough money. This goes for everyone, in my experience. Most won't break the law, and nor would I. Nor will I pay for the law to be broken. But I will pay for it to be bent. When I approach someone for a favour, before I offer them a cash incentive, I take their pulse, get to know them a little bit, and only then will I disclose what I need. I'll confide in them, telling them a little about me and my occupation, assuring them they'll never be exposed. Then I ask them their price. For this particular funeral worker, that figure was $500. So I knew the casket should be unlocked, and I knew how to open it. I also knew that what I was about to do wasn't going to go down well.

When I set my phone up with 'Pop Goes the Weasel' ready to play at the touch of a button, I had a rare moment of doubt. *Was this a little insensitive?* I wondered. For a second, my finger hovered over the button, but then I realised that I'd already promised the guy in the box I would do this; this wasn't my funeral, and therefore not my choice. *I'm the Coffin Confessor,* I thought. *Who am I to have feelings?*

As I entered the hall, I pressed 'play' on my phone and the song blasted out. I walked up to Marcus's coffin, grabbed the side and hoped like hell it'd actually open. Sure enough, *pop*, the lid came off and, sure enough, it was definitely Marcus inside. To be honest, he didn't look very well at all, and I understood why he'd wanted a closed casket – with a few precautions. I then closed the lid, glanced at the funeral director and gave him a nod. As I was leaving, a young bloke in a dark suit – my inside man – yelled out, 'Is he in there, mate? Hey mate, is Marcus in the coffin?'

In most cases, I have an 'inside man' (or woman) – a close family member, friend, or confidant of the deceased who knows

I'll be there. These people are necessary to keep me informed about my client's health, death and date and time of the funeral. They are also a legal witness to what follows, should anything go awry. It hasn't yet, but I make sure to dot every 'i' and cross every 't'. So they're in on it, but even they have no idea what I'll actually do to disrupt the funeral until I stand up. I also need these people to confirm I've done the job well.

I turned and gave him a nod and left with fucking 'Pop Goes the Weasel' still playing on my phone. I have to admit, while Marcus may have found the idea funny, I found it confronting. Maybe it was a bit too close to home. Sometimes I feel my life is in tune with that silly little song. Some days I'm fending off reporters, others I'm going on TV, or reading proposals and scripts, or getting excited by the prospects being brought to the table. But for some reason, when the music stops, the Coffin Confessor sometimes pops. In the back of my mind, I know that as my profile grows, it'll be harder and harder for me to serve clients like Marcus. His request would never have happened if the reporters who keep trying to find footage of me crashing a funeral had learned of it and crashed it themselves. At the same time, the media keeps raising awareness of my service, and I keep getting new requests I feel I have to honour. It's a self-fulfilling prophecy.

* * *

Probably the biggest media request I ever received was to do a TEDx event. I politely accepted, despite not knowing what the fuck a TEDx event was. After a Google search, I found out: TEDx is a world-famous series of short talks where experts in various fields share a bit of what they've learned. The events are held in front of a live audience, and they're also filmed and broadcast to millions of people around the world.

'TED' stands for 'Technology, Entertainment, Design'. I wasn't sure which of those the TEDx producers had filed me under – perhaps something got seriously lost in translation – but I'd already said yes and the thought of standing on a stage in front of a large audience got me excited. Only problem was those running the event wanted to know what I was going to talk about, down to the very last word. They asked for a script and asked me to memorise it. Standard procedure for them.

Not for me.

Reading and writing are skills that came to me late in life. I only learned to read because I wanted to get a driver's licence. So I can do it just fine now, but if I had to recite a script on stage, it would be halting and boring. Not having been educated to a standard that most are accustomed to prevented me from following the organisers' instructions. But I'd never let my education hold me back before, and it wouldn't now. These sorts of challenges have never stopped me from doing anything, and speaking at a TEDx event was just another one of those things I was going to do the only way I knew how. And that was prepare as best I could and then wing it.

As the event drew near, I received more and more calls from the organisers, increasingly worried that I wasn't ready for the big day. Nothing could have been further from the truth. Or could it? I knew the day and time I was set to speak. From my perspective, that's all I needed to know. Exactly *what* I'd say, well, that was anyone's guess.

We went back and forth for a while, the organisers insisting they needed a script to make sure that my talk was going to be entertaining, educational and informative. Fuck me if it wasn't all that and more; I gave the audience *exactly* what they needed, and while the organisers were surprised, I wasn't. I improvised a bit, but I got a standing ovation. TEDx doesn't pay a speaker's fee, so it's safe to say they got their money's worth. I was thrilled to have had the opportunity and was very grateful. It was such an awesome event, and the vibes on the day were incredible.

This 'say yes' philosophy has taken me to some interesting places, including being featured in a magazine I hadn't looked at since I was a teenager – *Penthouse*.

While having breakfast with Lara along the esplanade in Surfers Paradise one morning, I received a call from a journo at the girlie mag asking if I was available for a story. *And* a photo shoot. Immediately my mind went to the fully naked women featured in the centrefolds, which were among the most coveted items you could find in prison. People say they read these rags for the articles, but I can tell you that in Boggo Road Gaol that was a massive exaggeration. I'd not thought about *Penthouse* since leaving Boggo, but when I got the call that morning, my face must have flushed red because Lara gave me a puzzled look from over her eggs. 'Who was that?'

'*Penthouse* magazine,' I said. 'They want me for a centrefold!'

Lara laughed, thinking I was joking. 'Well, you might be about to get your first request for a refund.'

'I'm not joking. *Penthouse* wants to do an interview *and* a photo shoot.'

Breakfast was a bit surreal that morning, a married couple

in their fifties sipping coffee and discussing how one of them was going to appear in a men's magazine. It was something we both felt apprehensive about, but we went and looked at a copy (honestly, for the articles) and found that *Penthouse* had changed a great deal in thirty years.

In the end, I appeared not as the centrefold but in a three-page exposé in the winter edition, something I was quite chuffed about. Lara and I were both happy I kept my clothes on. And so were the magazine's readers and subscribers.

* * *

When I became a global phenomenon, it took some time for people to get their heads around the whole funeral-crashing concept, especially those with different religious backgrounds or who held different beliefs about death. However, once they realised that my crashing funerals and disclosing dirty little secrets was done at the request of the deceased – not a relative, friend, or enemy – they usually understood.

Even with my newfound celebrity status, not every appearance was pleasant. Late one afternoon I got a call from SBS inviting me to appear on *Insight*, a talkback style current affairs TV show. The format matched interesting guests with interesting topics in front of a live studio audience and put thorny questions to them to discuss. The theme of this particular show was 'Deathbed Confessions and Promises'. For me, it was a no-brainer, given that I'd already had a little bit of experience dealing with the media. But – and I don't say this very often – I was naive. Little did I know I was being set up.

As I sat among the other guests on the program, watching and listening to the presenter talk to a number of individuals about deathbed confessions, I could see I was surrounded by people who were compassionate yet held strong beliefs that funerals were for the living, not the deceased. Which is the opposite philosophy to mine, so I expected some tension. As the presenter turned to me, she said, 'Bill, you're a private investigator. You also call yourself the "Coffin Confessor", what do you . . .'

'In short, I crash funerals on behalf of the deceased,' I began. As I went on to elaborate, I could feel the crowd turning on me. I had no idea that I was going to be in a room full of people who were experienced and opinionated on death, and some of those death doulas were giving me looks. I could feel the daggers shooting from their eyes hitting my back live on air. The mumbles and groans about how disrespectful I was were just loud enough for me to hear, but I didn't care. All I could do was explain myself. Clearly, I'd been invited because I was supposed to give the villain edit on the program. The guy they bring in to say some controversial, contrarian shit so everyone has someone to hate. I guess it makes for good TV.

But the more I talked, the more people seemed to realise that I had honest intentions, and that I wasn't there with the express purpose of being a fuckwit. The presenter seemed to get it, even if a few of the other guests didn't.

I walked out feeling like I'd been set up. After the show, one audience member had a bit of a go, but I didn't sweat it. I get ambushed from time to time – somebody gets me on their show or podcast thinking they're going to confront me or get some kind of reaction out of me, but no chance. I very rarely let anything get to me. On this occasion, when this guy came at me with his criticisms, I simply said, 'Yeah, you could be right. I think you're wrong, but who cares? You do you, I'll do me. I crash funerals. You reckon I give a fuck what you think? I get paid to tell people to fuck off. This one's for free.'

And I walked off. After a minute or so, the guy called out, 'Hey, did you just tell me to fuck off?'

Sometime later, I went down to Sydney to film another, audio-only version of the show, and this time the producers were actually cool and curious about my work. There was a bit of a one-on-one beforehand. 'Did you feel as though we trapped you last time you came on the show?' they asked me.

'Fucking oath, I did! You guys set me up.' I said I had no fear of coming back and telling them exactly how I felt.

They'd done their homework this time and unbeknown to me, had spoken to a couple of people who'd been at funerals I'd crashed. I didn't know them from a bar of soap, because I don't keep film records of that part of my job. The producers were curious about why I didn't film the funerals I crashed, because that would be free advertising. 'Why would I do that?' I said. 'So they can end up all over the net? How does that keep the integrity of my contract with the clients? I have a contract with the client and that's it. Anybody who films me, great. I don't give a fuck what they do, but I don't film myself. That's not for me.'

Even so, the producers had tracked down a couple of people who'd witnessed me crashing funerals first-hand, and they got their take on it. And they had a psychologist who said that what I did was insensitive and sick.

'Yeah,' I said. 'But most psychologists are sick, so maybe they need help as well.'

I didn't mean to single out psychologists. Everyone needs help now and then. It's not going to kill you to see a psychologist, even if half of them are fucking crazy. I've had a few come out and say that I'm doing something brutal to the family. To which I say, 'I'm not there for the family. If telling the truth at the funeral is brutal for them, then the way they've treated the deceased during life is where the brutality started.'

I learned soon enough that the media can be brutal too, but it's a two-way street. I'm always happy to give my point of view. If people want to hear about what I'm doing, I'm happy to tell them. It's been very cool seeing requests come in from all over the world and I almost never turn them down, no matter how ruthless they are or whatever their agenda. Even when I know I'm walking into a trap, I usually go with it. I'm curious to see what they'll hit me with.

In fact, I've never cared what other people think or say about me. Especially when most say it behind my back or hide behind a keyboard. It's none of my business. Some might write to me with complaints and grievances, and I go, 'Oh, thank fuck, but we all have an expiration date. Holy shit. Why don't you let it go?'

I'm happy to just let it go. I don't have the time or the inclination to argue with everyone who has an opinion about me. It's the internet. Someone else will argue for you if you just wait a while. The cool thing is, every now and then I'll stumble across someone having a crack at me in the comments section, and then there'll be a bunch of comments below it defending me and my services. After the first time I got ambushed on TV I thought I'd be defending myself for the rest of my life, but other people were doing it for me. I can look in the comments section of a video and there'll be ten guys calling me a cunt, and another ten calling *them* cunts for being so small-minded. Which saves me a lot of time, and I appreciate it. While I know that arguing is what the internet is for, and you'll have two people in a conversation and three opinions, when I see that, I'm glad I started a conversation. Because in time, people really got behind the idea, including a couple with the keys to kick the whole thing up a gear.

* * *

When my story first went public, various publishers approached me to do a book. This wasn't something I expected for someone who'd gone half their life before starting their education. The publishers were all very nice, but there's a certain 'kind' of nice that has a little bit too much 'nice' to it, if you take my meaning. If I'm being wined (I rarely drink anything other than a nip of port) and dined (I like a nice steak dinner but can't be fucked with glamorous restaurants) then that's the wrong path to take. For that reason, it was my publisher from Penguin Random House Australia that I gravitated to. He didn't talk shit, didn't offer me lunch or dinner or glitz and glamour and all that bullshit. In fact, he was the only one who asked to hear my story – the one *behind* the headlines – not just the Coffin Confessor's. It was at that moment I knew who my publisher was going to be.

The book told the story of the rise of the Coffin Confessor, but also a little of the life of Bill Edgar, and how I'd got to that point. My past as a survivor of child sexual abuse. The years as a street kid and my incarceration for stealing a packet of cigarettes. As well as meeting the love of my life, Lara, starting a family, and building our life together. It was a raw, real book. After it came out, I had the weird experience of meeting people who knew everything about me.

'Fuck, you went through hell and back, good on you for surviving it,' one guy said to me at an event. 'I'm sorry you had such a fucked-up childhood.'

'Yeah,' is all you can really say to that. 'Me too.'

So I'm proud of that book for a lot of reasons, but out of all of them, the most important is the number of people who have reached out saying it inspired them to deal with their own history of abuse. It's never a burden when someone contacts me with their story. I always encourage them to act – to name and shame their abusers, no matter who it hurts. There might be some collateral damage, but abusers only survive because victims stay silent. You have to get it out there. No matter the price.

Of course, there are people who argue with that, and try to discredit me, and to them I say, I don't like your chances. Thanks to my first book, I have no secrets. I put everything that had ever happened to me in those pages; the good, the bad, the funny and the sad. That way the media couldn't dig up stories – they're already there. Some tabloid hack can't come out with a scoop that I'd been abused as a kid, or done time in prison, or been homeless, or anything else, because it's already on the record. I've had people come after me trying to dig up dirt, but none of them have been as good at the job as I am.

My own sister threatened to sell stories about me. I hadn't spoken to her in thirty years, no contact at all, but suddenly she

Going global

was on TikTok with a video saying that she had stories about 'her brother the Coffin Confessor' and she'd sell the rights to the highest bidder. I never replied. I thought, *Good on her, if she has any stories I haven't already told, good luck to her.* I didn't give her another thought after that. If I spend time thinking about those sorts of people it gives them space in my head, and they don't deserve that. I very rarely give a flying fuck what people think of me. But there have been times where the media intrusion has caused collateral damage.

* * *

I once did a podcast called *This American Life*. It's one of the biggest podcasts in the world, but I didn't know that at the time. From my point of view, I just got on a call, had a bit of a chat with a really cool interviewer somewhere in America, and then didn't think anything more of it. Until, that is, they asked to speak to someone who was at one of the funerals I'd crashed.

Against my better judgement, I connected them with Graham's daughter. Graham was the bloke whose joke inspired the Coffin Confessor and my first-ever crashed funeral. His daughter had been my 'inside woman', my contact within the family who Graham had told what I was going to do. At first she was hesitant, but the podcast producers promised her that she could stay anonymous, and so she agreed to do it.

But once the researcher knew Graham's daughter's identity, they tracked down all her friends and family who'd been at the funeral to get their opinion – and in doing so told them all that Graham's daughter had known I was going to crash it! Fucking abysmal behaviour, and the last thing Graham or his daughter would have wanted.

The family were enraged that she'd known I was going to crash the funeral and she'd done nothing to stop it. It didn't matter that it wasn't her choice, or that she would not have been able to stop me even if she'd tried. They didn't care about that. And they didn't care that it was Graham's idea in the first place. They turned on her and ostracised her from the family. A tragic, unfair outcome. For once I was too trusting, and the media too ruthless.

Around that time I realised I was in a bit over my head. I was receiving hundreds of requests for interviews, plus requests from producers, directors and storytellers all wanting to create a movie, television series, podcast or documentary. It was overwhelming, to be honest, and left me little time to do my actual job. But then, right on cue, I received a call from an agent in the US. His name was Steve Mandell. He was based in Chicago and said he'd seen me on a Chicago morning breakfast television show. He was so intrigued with what he saw he was compelled to get in touch and tell me he was going to be my agent.

At first, my reaction wasn't pleasant. I'd had a hundred calls from so-called agents, all of them talking shit, and I was put off by how confident and assured Steve sounded. So I was a bit of a prick to him, but he held his own, which I respected. He was a straight talker, a language I also spoke. Even if he did it in an American accent. Steve quickly convinced me he had the experience, expertise and professionalism to assist me, and truth be told I needed help. Things were getting crazy, the phone never stopped ringing and there were hundreds of emails that I couldn't reply to.

After speaking a few more times, I accepted his offer and was happy knowing he'd drive the media side of the Coffin Confessor. And even better, take care of the whole Hollywood side of things.

Working with Hollywood is not as fun as I thought it would be – its talk talk talk with little to nothing achieved. Then you wait days, weeks or even months for a reply. I've had some great conversations including one meeting with the comedian Marlon Wayans from the movie *White Chicks* about various people playing the role of the Coffin Confessor. But nothing's happened yet because Hollywood moves so slowly. But I'm fine with that, comfortable in the knowledge that Steve will handle all things media/television. I decided to keep a level head and not allow the hype of what's promised to consume me. I'm a realistic man and have always believed nothing's free, you don't spend what you don't have and if the money's not in the bank the deal ain't done.

* * *

So life was pretty good. I had a US agent, a publisher, a book, and the media at my beck and call. Nothing was going to slow me down. Except maybe the end of the world. Because just as this new adventure was getting underway, something was lurking around the corner, and it took me and pretty much everyone else by surprise. The dreaded COVID-19. The pandemic wreaked havoc and gave the average person a closer look at death than they probably ever expected. Which meant even more people reaching out to me and trying to understand what they were going through. I know it was a really tough time for most of the world, but for me the timing couldn't have been better. COVID-19 allowed me to slow down and take some time to think and reflect on what was important.

The flood of messages and emails became a torrent. People from all walks of life were telling me what they wanted to happen at their funeral; some even expressed their sorrow for not knowing of my service earlier, and that their loved ones would have loved to have used me to sort things out. Either to tell some people how much they were loved, or to tell the haters to fuck off. Others wrote and told me about their deathbed confessions.

Honestly, it's good to be recognised and known for what I do. At the same time it's so bizarre being the only person on the planet who seems to be doing it. I even got a letter from the bloody dictionary saying they were thinking of putting 'Coffin Confessor' in and could I help with a definition. Okay, why not?

It's cool, but I don't let it get to my head. If I was in my thirties I think it would have gone differently and I'd become an arrogant cunt, but I'm in my fifties. I'm more cautious and more aware of my priorities and what's important. At the end of the day, it's not about me. It's about the person who died and making their voice heard.

* * *

Nearly every week I think, *That's it, that was the last confession, it's over*, but every week someone new comes knocking and each time it's different. There are as many ways to die in this world as there are to live. Maybe more, really, because some people only muster the courage to be honest about how they want to live when they have one foot in the grave. Just as many spend their whole lives weighed down by regrets they just can't shake. Very different burdens to bear, but the result is the same – dying with a heavy heart, and enough of an urge to make things right, that they reach out to the Coffin Confessor as a last resort, to help them find peace.

3

Paid in full

'It was a fucking cold night,' Phillip recalled. 'I remember how cold it was, even for that part of the country.' It was late at night on a lonely road outside Orange, New South Wales, in the high country around 250 kilometres west of Sydney. At that altitude, winters have an edge to them. Orange is the only major city in Australia to see snowfall on a regular basis. The roads are tricky, especially when they are iced over.

That's why Phillip was taking extra care winding his Mack truck through the country, transporting a container of fresh produce. A young trucker of limited means, the midnight route brought in a bit of extra cash. Cold roads, cold air, so cold that Phillip had to crank the air con in the cabin to stop the windows fogging up. So cold that he didn't see the car wrecked by the side of the road until he was almost on top of it.

It was a Holden sedan, a good, solid car, but it was wrapped around a power pole like a scarf. Phillip slammed on the hydraulic brakes and pulled his truck up as close as he could get. The accident couldn't have happened long ago – steam was still billowing out of the Holden's radiator. It must have cracked, but no surprise there. The car was split practically in two. Through the window Phillip could see what looked like a human arm hanging limp through the wreckage of the car door. There was no movement from within the car.

No movement either on the road – no one coming or going along the long stretch of highway. It was a lonely road. A terrible place to have an accident. This was back before mobile phones, so Phillip called for help on his two-way radio. After speaking to several other truckers who relayed his call to emergency services, he was told that an ambulance and police were on their way.

So he grabbed his torch, got out of the truck and made his way to the wrecked car. What he thought was a human arm wedged in the mangled driver's side door was definitely that. It just wasn't attached to a body. The body it belonged to was in a ditch on the side of the road, where it must have been flung by the impact. Blood pooled under the body. There was blood everywhere. More blood than Phillip had ever seen, and he'd seen a lot. Before he became a trucker, he'd worked in an abattoir.

The Holden's driver was dead. His companion, a woman, was still in the passenger seat. Her seatbelt was on, but it hadn't helped. From the angle of her neck and the colour of her skin, Phillip could tell she was dead before he felt for her pulse. He checked anyway, leaning into the car. It seemed the woman had been going through her handbag at the time her companion had lost control. Her belongings were scattered everywhere. Lipstick, purse, money. A *lot* of money. A thick bundle of cash was lying on the floor, miraculously untouched by the blood. Phillip stared at the cash. He looked up and down the road, still deserted, still cold and fucking lonely. Not a soul for miles. No witnesses. Emergency services were on their way, but there was nothing they could do now except provide a hearse for this poor couple.

Phillip turned back to the money and made a choice. He put it in his pocket.

The money changed everything. Fast forward a few decades and Phillip's life was good. He was still a truck driver, but nowadays he owned the company he drove for. Money was not a problem, his health was fine, he had a great relationship with his wife and children. He had a reputation as a hard worker and a smart businessman. But he had this secret, and it was eating him up inside. For over thirty years he was sure that if he told anyone what he'd done that night it would destroy him – his integrity, his good standing, and everything he loved and had worked so hard for.

He never knew the names of the couple who'd been killed in the accident. In truth, he never *wanted* to know. He thought knowing their names would make what he'd done more personal. It'd make him feel even worse than he already did. Phillip tried desperately to erase it from his memory and as the years went by that's exactly what happened. He repressed the memory of that dead couple he'd stolen from and became a part-time philanthropist. He donated in excess of $250,000, paying it forward, to charities and soup kitchens, and even paying the rent, groceries and power bills that struggling people in his community couldn't afford themselves. His charity helped him live with what he'd done all those years ago.

For a while. Eventually, his demons caught up with him on another lonely road.

As the boss of his company, Phillip still loved driving trucks, but nowadays he could choose his routes, and rarely drove interstate. But through some wild twist of fate, he ended up driving a lovely road in a similar part of New South Wales, on another lonely night, when he came across another accident, and it all came back like it was yesterday.

It's common enough, especially for men of a certain generation. You can repress a trauma to the extent that you can carry on with life, but you never know when you'll experience something that will trigger a flashback so vivid that it can be emotional, confronting and controlling all at the same time.

The memories that seeing this latest accident brought back haunted Phillip, until they drove him to finally confront them. He decided it was time to find out the identities of the couple whose money he'd stolen. So he contacted me and engaged my services. Phillip was that rare client who approached me to settle matters of life and death when he himself was a long way from the grave. His physical health was fine. But the guilt was doing his head in, and he thought finding out who the couple were and making amends would stop them haunting him.

I was happy to help.

* * *

It didn't take me long to track down the details of the accident – two dead adults, one male, one female, single motor vehicle accident outside Orange. A white VL Commodore left the road at high speed hitting a power pole. The driver was suspected of falling asleep at the wheel. Their names were easy to find. From there, a routine investigation locating people who had known them uncovered their story.

Josh and Izzy were middle-aged sea changers who'd arrived from South Africa to settle in Broome, Western Australia, where they bought and ran a small diving boat business. They'd bought the business before they migrated, but they soon found themselves disappointed. After a few months, they decided to pack up shop and travel around Australia, basically wherever the winds took them. While they didn't have a set destination or any special plans, Izzy was eager to explore, so that's how they ended up just outside Orange in New South Wales.

Unfortunately, that's where the travels ended for Josh and Izzy.

But not for Phillip.

After telling him all this, he took a few minutes to process it. He asked if the couple had any surviving family, and if leaving anything to them would help.

I answered carefully. 'The family was well off. I don't think the money would have made a big difference to their grief.' In my view, tracking them down and confessing to the theft would only bring more pain.

The fact that he'd kept the memory of Josh and Izzy's lonely death alive all these years, and assisted so many in paying it forward, was a much better way to remember the dead. 'Honestly, I believe you've done enough. You can only fix what you can fix, and the accident wasn't your fault. Maybe it's time for you to put it to rest.'

* * *

I meant it. I've heard all types of stories and seen all types of things and it takes a lot to shock me. Honestly, Phillip stealing from two victims when he was the first responder to an accident was an appalling act. I wonder how many people have been in a similar situation and had to live with that sort of guilt. Not many, I hope.

I'll never forget being the first responder to an accident when I was working as a removalist in my early twenties. My colleague and I came across a car that had hit a power pole. As we rushed to help we could see two elderly people inside the vehicle, a male driver and a female passenger. My colleague ran around to the passenger side and tried to assist the woman, who was bleeding from her forehead. He then tried to help the driver by giving him CPR. Unfortunately, the man was beyond help. Maybe that memory sticks out for me because it was the first time I'd had somebody die in my arms. I can't imagine that if I'd noticed a pile of cash in the car I would have snatched it. If you were to ask me about the colour of the car or if I saw a wallet, a handbag or any other valuable item I couldn't tell you; my focus was solely on the man and the woman.

So I didn't exactly approve of Phillip's actions, but he was just a kid. Thirty years and a quarter of a million dollars is more than enough to spend on a guilty conscience.

I know all too well what it's like to live with guilt. When I was a street kid I stole, lied and cheated every chance I got in order to survive. Money meant the difference between having a full belly and a safe place to sleep or taking my chances on the underbelly of the Gold Coast. Theft was my only way to get money then, and there have been occasions since where I've slipped.

Over the years, raising two children and working odd jobs with never enough cash, I occasionally thought about stealing, and a few times thoughts turned into action. I recall one afternoon after Lara and our newborn son had just moved into a caravan park. I had a job at a local Shell service station pumping fuel, checking tyres and cleaning windshields. The service station also had a car wash and I'd often be called upon to detail a car or two. I couldn't help but feel jealous when I'd be sweating my guts out cleaning some rich person's weekend drive and seeing how carelessly they left their valuables and cash lying around.

For the price of just one of those luxury cars, Lara and I could have put a deposit on a home and gotten ourselves out of precarious housing. It was a real kick in the guts to go from scrubbing a Mercedes to counting our change in the supermarket and realising we could afford nappies for our baby, or food, but not both.

One day I snapped. I decided it was time to improve our financial situation. I crept out late at night, leaving Lara and our baby fast asleep, and walked the streets of the suburb of Ashmore. I noticed a man and woman getting into a car parked in the driveway of a luxury home. They drove away, leaving the house unattended. They were dressed fancy – for a long night out – and it was at that moment that I knew my target.

As I waited for the car to disappear down the street I scanned the neighbours' houses for activity. There was nothing that gave me any cause for alarm. No lights or evening strollers, the only dog I could hear barking was at least ten houses away.

First, I tried the garage door. Locked. The front door was locked too, as was the back door. But from the backyard, I noticed a bathroom window that wasn't shut properly. Quickly,

I climbed through and gained my composure, then took some time exploring my new surroundings. My first target was the master bedroom. As I opened the large, mirrored wardrobe I could see a variety of men's and women's clothing all hanging in a neat row. Below the clothes were expensive-looking shoes. More women's than men's and all high-quality brands. I started looking inside the jackets, handbags and purses for valuables, but found nothing.

Then I looked above the clothes and noticed a number of hats. Under one of the hats was a small bag, and inside that bag were three rolls of banknotes. I quickly counted about $4000. I took half and left half, bundling it as I found it: $2000 was a life-changing amount of money, and I figured the theft would be less likely to be noticed in a hurry. I also found a small bag of powder and a pipe – something that didn't interest me – so I put the bag back where I found it, closed the wardrobe and left the way I came in.

As I walked back to Lara and bub I started to have regrets. Not about crossing the line into burglary, but for not going further. Maybe I should have taken the lot? What was another $2000 to a couple of rich junkies when I had a hungry baby at home? Fuck me I was confused, often stopping along the way, thinking about going back, but with every step closer to home I knew I had all I needed.

When I arrived back at the caravan park Lara and bub were fast asleep, none the wiser. It was only years later that I would confess to Lara what I had done that night.

* * *

I usually stole because my life depended on it, or I needed food, or a roof over my head and clothing, but I always knew karma would one day come knocking. Because these memories were a burden, more and more as life went on, and especially since my thirties, I've tried to pay it forward by helping people whenever I can. I've even found some of those I hurt and stole from and paid them back in full. As an experienced PI, it was easy enough for me to track people down and pay them back in both money and sincere apologies.

While it's no secret I've hunted down and confronted those who've hurt me, it's coming face to face with those *I* hurt that I've found the most difficult. It's not that easy to find a random couple who have moved houses several times in the intervening years, knock on their door, and politely say, 'Hello, I'm very sorry, but when I was younger I stole half of your drug money to feed my baby.'

So it took time to find and repay everyone I could remember stealing from. Eventually, I settled the whole ledger, except for one who continued to elude me. When I was just sixteen years old I stole $5000 in cash from a wealthy schoolmate, Anthony. I drained his account via a bug in the ATM's withdrawal system. Anthony was a rich kid, with a rich kid's naivety, and even though I really liked him, I took advantage of that.

Anthony and his parents knew it was me all along, but the police couldn't charge me because there was no evidence, and they had no idea how a snotty-nosed street kid was capable of stealing money from an ATM, and I wasn't about to tell them. At the time I was proud of a fairly sophisticated system I'd worked out to hack and steal from ATMs. As time passed, that pride turned into something closer to shame.

It would be years before I tried to find Anthony and when I did it wasn't easy. During my searches I stumbled upon his son who told me Anthony had succumbed to brain cancer some ten years earlier. I told his son what I was hoping to achieve, and that I wanted to pay him the money back in full, which rightfully belonged to the family. While he was sympathetic and understanding I could tell he was also somewhat disappointed that a friend had taken advantage of his dad. I didn't ask for his forgiveness.

With Anthony dead, it was too late to seek his forgiveness for what I'd done. The only person in the equation who could forgive me, was me. That's the only way to really cleanse yourself of that kind of guilt – finding a way to self-forgiveness. It provided a cleansing and solace in my life, even if it only happened much later on. That's what I hoped to pass on to Phillip when we closed his case. Self-forgiveness, solace; it's powerful and in many ways is the opposite of revenge.

I think it's helped me to become a better person. As the Coffin Confessor, I work with people who are, if they're not already, so frail and confused they would be easy to take advantage of. I have the opportunity to steal from those who depend on me or those who have already stepped through death's door, but the thought of doing so has never entered my mind. I get paid very well for what I do, and my integrity is everything. While I might be an atheist I am somewhat spiritual and even I know stealing from the dead is as bad as it gets. Karma is a one mean lady, and now that I'm a little wiser, I don't fuck around with her.

* * *

Although I have a policy of offering my services to anyone who needs them regardless of my own moral stance, there are certain lines I will not cross. I don't break the law – especially not if someone is watching – and I always act in a way that is going to settle karma, instead of kicking it up.

I once said I would never refuse a request from the dying, but this wasn't a request from someone who was dying. Nor was she terminally ill or even poorly. Jill, a middle-aged woman who was due to attend her father's funeral in the coming days, wanted to expose the man for who he really was. Jill told me she'd been raped and molested by her father. Every time she tried to speak about it she would shake uncontrollably. She wouldn't dare stand up and expose him for the monster he was, especially at his funeral, but she knew what I was capable of. She also knew that as an abuse survivor myself, I had skin in the game, as I always try to name, shame and bring abusers to justice.

However, as a private investigator I need to know the facts. Jill's case was no different. She had my sympathies, she was clearly troubled, but just telling me she was raped and molested by her father wasn't enough for me to crash his funeral and rain down the collateral damage that it would bring to her family.

I understand what it's like to be a victim of child abuse. I was abused at home and school from the age of seven. I shouted my abuse from the rooftops but no one listened. They called me a liar, but I wouldn't allow myself to live in silence. But I understand why so many victims do until they meet someone who sets an example of how to speak up.

Fear has a way of stopping us from having fun, taking a leap of faith, jumping out of an aeroplane and even exposing those who hurt and torment us. It's fear that keeps most victims silent; fear of being called a liar, or being ridiculed, or ostracised. But not me. I lived in fear my whole childhood and I have no fear left. And there's nothing more dangerous than a person who has no fear. No matter how big or small they are, the fearless will always win.

The night before my eighth birthday my grandfather sexually attacked me. The next morning I was given a bike and my mother hit me with the kettle cord because I didn't show any gratification or love towards my grandfather who'd bought me the bike. That was the day fear found me. It took nine years of being continually abused not only by him but by my teachers at school until fear finally left and I confronted him about it. I nearly killed him but stopped right on the precipice. On that day, I lost the ability to feel fear. But when you lose fear you lose the ability to care and on some occasions the ability to know when to stop. Caution is something I had to learn, and I knew enough to use it here.

I investigated Jill's claims and got to know her father as best I could without ever setting eyes on him. He was too far gone for me to interview him, so I did a thorough background check – canvassing official records, every paper trail, and every person I could find to get a read on the man. To be honest, I couldn't find anything that made me think Jill's allegations were credible. I couldn't find any criminal records or anything that led me to factual evidence. Jill had no health records to support her claims – no GP visits, no rape kits, no history of seeing mental health professionals about the abuse. None of this made for conclusive evidence. Plenty of victims can't produce evidence of their abuse, which is part of the reason they stay silent.

Despite a thorough investigation, the worst thing I could find about Jill's father was that he was a masochist and frequented a dominatrix who would punish him and tell him all types of shit that got him off sexually. Personally, it's not something I've ever explored. The last thing I'd want is to stand naked in front of a woman and be punished, bashed or attacked, but to each their own. So that was it: a fairly harmless secret kink between consensual adults. Probably something he should have had a conversation with his wife about, but not proof of abuse.

It was finally time to sit down with Jill and have a difficult conversation. I told her that without solid proof of her allegations I couldn't in good conscience take her on as a client, unless her father himself hired me. She was upset, but she didn't argue. My read on the situation was that while Jill clearly *had* suffered some kind of trauma, she was, as she hinted, fabricating the allegations against her father. Why, I'll never know. She clearly had a lot going on mentally, more than I could reasonably help her with, and so I wished her well and went on my way.

Some clients feel I'm not working in their best interests, given I'll expose secrets and lies. A lot of the time, these are told by the client as a means to win my sympathy. Nine times out of ten, if a client hires me to expose some wrongdoing in their life, it started with something fucked up they did to the person who wronged them, long ago. I'm thorough and won't leave a stone unturned, even if that means upsetting the very person who's engaged my services. Sometimes I feel bad that I have to turn down and upset a potential client. But I'm never surprised when someone full of righteous anger turns out to have more skeletons in the closet than they let on.

* * *

When I met Leon I wasn't so much shocked as I was enraged by what he told me. In February 2022, while living his last days in aged care in country Victoria, he sent me a handwritten letter telling me about his life. It was coming to an end now, and he had engaged a lawyer to settle his estate and divide the money up to causes he felt most deserved them. He had no living relatives that he knew of, except for a nephew named Gabriel, who he hadn't seen in over forty years and had no fondness for. Despite this, the lawyer told him to leave at least 5 per cent of his estate to Gabriel as this would deter the nephew from contesting the will. Leon's lawyer even went to the trouble of finding Gabriel and telling him about his long-lost uncle. He did this without Leon's consent. This is something I found fucking impossible to understand. The only explanation is that it would benefit the lawyer, because he must have worked out a way to skim a few extra dollars from the whole thing. Since I'm not a lawyer I can tell the truth and say I have little to no trust in the blood-sucking parasites, especially where money is concerned.

Leon told me he wanted to donate all of his estate to charity and that if his nephew were to contest his will then the Coffin Confessor was to intervene. I couldn't do anything about the legal side of things, which was being manipulated by the lawyer, so Leon wanted me to hunt Gabriel down and make his life a living hell.

This was a tricky one. On one hand, it sounded like something I'd have no problem doing. In the event of this long-lost nephew grabbing at a dying man's money, my moral compass was pointing very strongly towards me finding Gabriel (and the lawyer) and scaring the living shit out of them both. But that wasn't something I could do given the legalities. I decided instead to write back to Leon letting him know my concerns, not only with taking revenge against the long-lost nephew, but also with his lawyer. I suggested he get another lawyer to look over everything. That's where the rot had begun in the first place, I suspected. But that's all I could do. Leave it to the law, and worse, the lawyers. Sometimes, the best thing to do by a client is to leave them be, and not make things worse by intervening. Take Bianca, for example.

* * *

In August 2021 I met Bianca, a woman who had been following me on social media. She emailed me asking if we could meet face to face as she was travelling from New Zealand to the Gold Coast. I agreed.

It was late on a Thursday afternoon when I met her at a bar in Hope Island – a suburb that has become a place for the class just above middle but not yet at the top. If you believe the bullshit real-estate people say about suburbs, this was one of the ones you live in to show you are affluent. Or is that effluent? I can never remember how to tell them apart.

Bianca was in her fifties, married with five children and a number of grandchildren. She lived in New Zealand but two of her kids and her mother lived near the Gold Coast, so she visited frequently. Our conversation started with the usual small talk – weather, family, and her flight to Australia – but once she became comfortable enough she explained why she wanted to meet.

Bianca told me how she had lost her father in a motorbike accident several years earlier. This took a great toll on her mother, but she would be provided for materially. Like most husband-and-wife wills, after the funeral affairs were settled, Bianca's mother would inherit everything she and her husband had built together over the past fifty or more years.

Bianca then told me how her sister had tried to access part of their father's estate by hiring a lawyer. She'd been unsuccessful and the legal challenge had amounted to nothing, but Bianca's mother was now gravely ill, and Bianca expected her sister to launch another legal attack. This meant the whole family was about to endure another shit show, something Bianca was hoping to avoid. This was why she sought my help.

Given the nature of wills and estates, Bianca needed someone with a little more knowledge and experience than me, and so I gave her some contacts hoping this would be the end of our meeting. But it wasn't. Bianca didn't just want justice; she wanted revenge. She wanted to hire me to crash her mother's funeral and expose her sister for the piece of shit that Bianca believed she was.

'I can't do that,' I said. I don't work for third parties, only for the client who has directly hired me. If I'm going to crash a funeral you can be sure I've been hired by the now deceased person – not their relatives, friends or associates. I explained my role and how it all works and Bianca decided it would be best for me to meet her mother so as she could engage my services first-hand.

And so, about a week later, I found myself in a nursing home in Southport. When I arrived, Bianca was already waiting for me in the lobby. As we walked towards her mother's room I asked her what to call her mother.

'Vera,' said Bianca. 'Her name is Vera.'

Vera was a name I'd only ever heard once before. This was when I was a street kid and met a New Zealand lady by the same name who treated me very kindly. She and her husband saw I was living rough, and were very generous, giving me food and money. They didn't have much themselves, but they shared what they could, and I was very grateful for their handouts. Perhaps for this reason, I felt warmly towards Vera, even though we'd never met.

As we reached her room I introduced myself and smiled politely all the while looking deep into her eyes. I could tell she didn't have long to go. I always know when someone is not long for this world. I can see the colour of death in a person. There'll be a grey, slightly orange tinge to their eyes. As I stood by Vera's bed, I found it hard to comprehend what she was saying. Bianca was trying to interpret for me, but I could tell even Bianca was having problems understanding her mother.

After a few minutes Vera fell asleep and in a low tone I whispered to Bianca, 'Let's leave her to sleep and get something from the café.' I told Bianca I'd meet her there as I needed to go to the bathroom. Not to go to the toilet but to splash water on my face and gain some composure. I just knew Bianca was going to come at me strongly with her requests. And that those requests were *her* wishes, not her mother's.

When I got to the café Bianca had already ordered two coffees. As I sat down to discuss the situation she said she had the money to pay me now, up-front, no questions asked. I declined the payment, telling her that I believed her mother was too far gone to engage my services. Vera wasn't capable of sitting up and focusing on a discussion, let alone making a decision to hire the Coffin Confessor and potentially ruin her funeral.

Bianca became upset at this. 'Something needs to be done about my sister. What's your problem?'

'I can't do this for you. But you can,' I said, softly but firmly. 'If you have a truth to say at your mother's funeral, then you should find the courage to come out and say it yourself.'

'That's impossible. The whole family would turn against me.' She thought for a second. 'I'll give you another grand. A thousand on top of the asking price.'

'It's not about the money,' I said. I explained that it was about what her mother truly wanted, and my role and dignity as the Coffin Confessor. Something that couldn't be bought.

'Motherfucker,' Bianca muttered under her breath.

Either she wanted me to hear it, or it just slipped out. Either way, I understood. She was frustrated and angry, but if her mother wasn't capable of engaging my services then unfortunately our time was up.

I stood and said goodbye, but before I left Bianca pleaded with me once more to help her. There was nothing I could do. As I walked off, again I heard her calling me a name. This time it was 'cunt'. I didn't break my stride. This wasn't the first time, nor would it be the last that I've been given that title. Honestly, it was a bit of an honour to be called that by Bianca. It told me I'd made the right choice in refusing her request.

A few days later I received a text from Bianca telling me her mother had passed away and that her cousin was going to crash the funeral. Bianca suggested that he might become the latest Coffin Confessor and I'd be out of a job. Perhaps she was hoping that I'd changed my mind but I hadn't. I replied, 'My deepest sympathy for your loss and I hope your cousin can pull it off.'

Two weeks later I received another text from Bianca. She said her cousin freaked out and decided to remain seated, unable to crash his Aunt Vera's funeral. I knew that he would.

What I do isn't for everyone. There's a reason for that. You need a certain kind of temperament. That's no secret. The real secret to the job is knowing when to do nothing at all.

* * *

I suspected that if Bianca had found a way to convince me to confront her sister, she would have regretted it soon enough. Anger and vengeance are terrible ways to solve your problems, especially when family and impending death are involved.

I can't remember many occasions where angrily confronting someone has made the situation better. It feels good in the moment, but later on, when the adrenaline has faded and you're trying to get the bloodstains out of your shirt, you feel terrible. I've found it much more satisfying to confront those who have wronged me with quiet dignity. It does far more damage to a paedophile hiding behind a teacher's desk to stand in their doorway in front of their family and say, 'Do you remember me? Do you remember what you did to me?' And then walk away knowing they'll have to live with themselves. That's revenge enough.

When I first started out as the Coffin Confessor I had a lot of requests from people who wanted some kind of revenge after they died. Bitterness against people who did not visit them on their deathbed, or who did not behave how they thought was appropriate in life. But as it grew, I saw less and less of that, and more people seeking solace rather than revenge.

In their final hours, it's very rare I meet someone who's fuelled entirely by revenge. Who pays ten grand for an act of revenge they're never going to see? The motivation is different – it's a way for people to cleanse themselves by getting rid of all the shit they could never say or do in life. Revenge offers no solace at the end of the day. But unburdening does.

Human beings are such fuck-ups that if you just wait a while, your worst enemy will usually sort themselves out, because they are their own worst enemy too. That's all I can really tell the Biancas of the world. Revenge doesn't help. We've all met people you'd fucking never want to talk to again, and maybe who you'll hate forever. Does that mean you should take revenge on them? No. It just means that you should let it go. And move on.

4

Material girl

It was early 2022 when Paula contacted me from the oncology ward of the Royal North Shore Hospital in Sydney. In her twenties or early thirties, she had cancer and the prognosis wasn't good. She was initially treated as an outpatient, while living with her housemate in a glamorous beachside suburb.

While her housemate was away, Paula had a severe reaction to one of her medications, and had been rushed to hospital by ambulance. Her admission had been so quick that she had only the clothes on her back, and her phone. And she only managed to charge her phone because a nurse loaned her a charger. Paula used it to call me. She sounded sick, but upbeat and cheerful. She asked me to go to her apartment, gather up her personal items – most importantly her computers, cameras and assorted media devices – and bring them to her in the oncology ward. This was when COVID-19 was still lingering around like a bad smell, and access to hospitals was highly restricted. Paula needed someone who could get around all of that and get her items to her. By coincidence, I happened to be going to Sydney at the time, so I agreed to help her, after some routine research and background checks.

That was easy enough. Paula was a professional influencer. That is, someone, usually a glamorous young woman, who has a large social media presence and sells that to companies to spruik their goods or services. Influencers are everywhere these days – if you've been to a holiday resort in the past five years, you will have seen them taking selfies, talking to themselves while they film little videos, or striking poses while a very bored boyfriend holds the camera. It's a legitimate career path for kids these days. Which seems fucking crazy to a guy like me who grew up when the internet was still a twinkle in a nerd's eye, but there you go. Influencers can make good money, and there are lots of them out there, aspiring to be sent products to review and advertise. I've even heard about teenagers pretending they have sponsorship from brands because it's a status symbol.

As is the number of 'friends' or 'followers' you have online. The fact that friendship, that relationships, that your own personal fucking identity is something that can be measured and packaged and sold is a total nightmare for a new generation. And the fact that it's widely accepted that the way you get on in the world is to turn yourself into a living advertisement? Well, that's just brutal.

Paula, at least, appeared to be a fairly successful influencer. She had tens of thousands of followers on her social media accounts, which were packed with photos of her posing in exotic hotels, dressed in high-end fashions, expensive hair and makeup. She looked like a million bucks.

When I located and let myself into her unit, it was bare, and I mean it had only the bare essentials: a bean bag for sitting in, a small television and a futon bed all in the lounge. In the kitchen there was very little to see other than a blender and a conventional oven, but the bedroom was another story. It was a studio with a green screen, cameras, lights and microphones – all high-end gear. There were a number of scripts plastered to the walls and the back of the door so they could be easily read. There were also boxes and wrapping paper and numerous unopened items such as shampoo, tinting shit, hairspray and make-up. Fuck me if this chick didn't live an extreme life of fake, false, pretentious shit all funded by companies that cared more about their products being exploited than they were about her.

I went and collected her items from her apartment and brought them to her ward. The hospital was still in a state of high biosecurity, so your average person would have found it near impossible to get in. But, as always, if you know the right palm to grease, any door can be opened. I made contact with a guy I knew from when we'd both worked nightclub security in Cairns. He'd moved up in the world, and he was now part of the security management team that provided specialist security to certain government organisations, including hospitals. His assistance was most welcome, and well rewarded.

I made my way up to Paula's floor. She was lying in a hospital bed, but she was ready for a guest. Somehow, in the middle of an oncology ward it seems, she'd found a make-up artist and a hair stylist. She looked like she'd just come from the salon and greeted me by asking if I wanted a selfie with her.

'No thank you,' I said. 'Would you like one with me?' I meant it in a friendly way, but she didn't take too kindly to my reply. She lay back on the bed and pouted, as though I'd insulted her. We didn't get off to a great start but we talked a little, and I admit that I felt for her. It was clear that she was embarrassed to be sick. This was around March 2022, and her cancer diagnosis was not good. Best-case scenario, she'd make it to Christmas.

I agreed to be her Coffin Confessor. This meant making sure her final message was delivered at her funeral and her last social media posts went up. In the meantime, she wanted me to get around hospital security and bring her more devices and all the shit that she needed to continue her work. This meant smuggling in the merchandise, clothes and beauty products that companies kept sending her. She had around twenty different luxury brands posting her shit every week, paying good money so that she'd feature it in her glamorous lifestyle posts.

I couldn't believe it. She was in this grey oncology ward, palliative care machines beeping all around her, a drip in her arm, and she was taking calls with brand ambassadors from high-end fashion labels. The whole time her cancer advanced, she was posting photos and videos of herself carefully shot so that she looked to be at home, reviewing a new bag or lipstick or brand of weight-loss herbal tea or whatever the fuck. Paula didn't need weight-loss herbal tea. She was on chemotherapy.

When she got too sick to fake even that, she kept posting photos that she'd stored of her posing in Versace and in fancy hotel rooms. The sicker she became, the harder she worked trying to show the world that she was fine. That everything was rosy and she was in another fucking dimension.

Material girl

I couldn't understand it. It's like she'd been so brainwashed by the need for glamour and validation from strangers that she'd become a product herself. She could no sooner stop reviewing handbags than she could breathing, because if she wasn't the product anymore, what was she? Her status and social standing were more important to her than anything else, right down to the last breath.

Sadly, Paula didn't make it to Christmas. When she died, her social circle was non-existent. Only seven people attended her funeral (to be fair, it was during COVID-19), even though the post announcing her death attracted thousands of likes, shares and messages of condolences.

* * *

Out of all the weird and fucked-up things I've seen as the Coffin Confessor, this one really disturbed me. Imagine being on your deathbed and being worried not about dying, but about your appearance?

I know this will sound hypocritical coming from a former *Penthouse* pet (technically true), but looks aren't everything. I've spent enough time in aged care homes and hospitals to know that at the end of the road we all end up looking pretty shit, so why worry about it now? When you hit fifty, you'll look back on photos of yourself and realise just how lucky you had it when you were young, before the body starts creaking and falling apart, and maintenance becomes pretty much a full-time job.

I'm in my fifties now, and I think to myself how lucky I am that I have my health. I don't take it for granted, and make sure I invest in it first and foremost. That doesn't mean following strict diets or running marathons. Just a forty-minute workout most days and a balanced diet. Everything in moderation. Even moderation on special occasions, because you have to enjoy life.

I find it deeply weird that young people spend so much time worrying about their appearance, or whether they're cool enough in the eyes of their peers, or their status in society. It's so much worse now with social media. It's such a waste of time. At the end of the day – at the end of a battle with cancer – we all look the same. And we all have the same regrets.

The deathbed confessions I've heard all come in different wrappings, but once you get down to it, the same few things appear over and again. One of the major ones is spending time worrying about what other people think of you. The other major one is wasting a life trying to accumulate material possessions, losing sight of what's important, and realising only too late what really matters.

I've never been a materialistic person. Sure, I've wanted things, and I have possessions that I enjoy owning. But they're not my priority in life by a long fucking way. I've got a roof over my head, and my family, and that's all I really need. The rest is a bonus. As long as I have my integrity I'm quite happy with who I am and where I'm going. I run my own race and no one else's. And I'm definitely not running into the grave. I'm tiptoeing. Very slowly. While not letting possessions weigh me down. After all, you can't take them with you.

* * *

Benny was a client who knew that he couldn't take his possessions with him but wanted to try anyway. Strangely enough, a bit like Paula, he wanted me to bring him his phone. He was terrified of being buried alive and wanted a safeguard so he could make an emergency call from the grave. It's a common enough fear – a friend of mine once tasked me to prick his body with a pin at his funeral to make sure he was really dead.

Benny didn't want me to touch his body at all, but wanted his fully charged mobile placed alongside his body where the funeral director wouldn't find it. If Benny somehow woke up in the grave, he'd be able to make a call.

I've been asked to place all sorts of things in coffins and graves and the most common item is the mobile phone. For what rhyme or reason I don't know. It may be the comfort of knowing no one is going to access it and discover your secrets. Or perhaps the deceased think they may miraculously come back to life after they've been buried and they'll need to tell someone about it. Not that they'll have much reception six feet under but at least they'll have a torch and some memorable photos to scroll through. I know at least one woman who's no longer with us who would have given anything to be able to post one last selfie.

Benny's reason was straightforward, and it should have been a simple enough job. After his death, I attended the viewing for friends and family, slipped the phone into his coffin, and was about to make my getaway when the fucking thing started ringing. What a disaster. I think Benny would have approved.

Benny was a character. Everything was a joke to him, even life and death. If you asked him what he thought about his imminent demise he'd shrug and say, 'It is what it is,' and truth be told, it was what it was. His outlook on life was what you'd expect from someone from Darwin, in the top end of Australia. Someone who went fishing and camping most of his life, wrestled a croc or two, loved a drink and could tell a yarn that had you hanging on his every word. The sort of stories you can't write down, because you need your hands to properly tell the tale and demonstrate how he caught a fish 'this big'.

I met Benny at the casino on the Gold Coast, and he was a fish out of water if ever there was one. He'd read my first book and decided that while he was in town attending his niece's graduation party, he had to meet me and talk about his final requests. We agreed to meet at the casino's sports bar. I told him what colour shirt I'd be wearing. He told me to look out for the loudest guy in the place wearing a hat that looked like it had been eaten, chewed and spat out by a croc. It didn't take me long to single him out. In fact, he got my attention by noticing me first and yelling out, 'Confessor mate! Here's Benny!' Fuck me if he wasn't loud and embarrassing but at the same time very likeable.

He told me about his health issues. He had less than a year to live and had decided he was going to make the most of it rather than getting treatment that might prolong his time on earth, but would diminish his quality of life. I admired him for that.

After discussing life, death and everything in-between, Benny engaged my services and briefed me on how he wanted the mobile phone placed in his coffin. I was a little dismayed at him handing me a brand-new phone long before he was due to die. It seemed like a waste. If I was being buried, I'd be happy with an old burner phone as long as it booted up, but hey, it's the client's dollar not mine.

Benny said he'd transferred photos and a few private documents onto this particular phone and wanted it placed discreetly in the coffin. He also told me he had left instructions with his niece to notify me of his passing and date of the viewing. He seemed pretty happy when he told me all this. Most people find deathbed confessions and instructions empowering. It's as though they feel somewhat in control, and I love being a part of that.

Two days after Christmas in 2022 I received the call that Benny had just passed away and arrangements were being made for his viewing and funeral. The first viewing would be held in four days and his funeral in six. With that news, I booked my ticket to Darwin.

When I arrived I made my way to the address I'd been given and found a number of people already gathered. Some waited outside the viewing hall, others wandered around inside, but all shared a sombre look on their faces. Which didn't seem like how the Benny I met would like to be remembered, but it wasn't my place to say. My job was easy. Or it should have been.

I waited for a bit before asking one of the ushers for a private viewing. I was given three minutes. I really only needed thirty seconds to hide the phone inside Benny's coffin, but hey, while I had the time I may as well say my goodbyes to a bloke who seemed larger than life. 'I know you might not be able to hear me, mate, but I've done what you asked, and I can only hope you're in a better place. If you're not, I know you'll make the most of it. See you later, Benny, it was a pleasure to meet you.'

A minute later the door to the viewing room opened. The usher came in to discreetly signal that my viewing time was over. 'Are you okay?' she asked, testing to see if I was in need of comfort.

'Would you like a box of tissues or a glass of —' Mid-sentence she was cut off, when the fucking mobile phone I left in Benny's coffin started ringing. The usher and I looked at each other for a long moment while the phone continued to ring. I have to say, she'd turned a strange colour.

'Oh no,' I said, quickly retrieving the mobile from the casket. 'I must have dropped it!' The usher made herself scarce. The phone was still ringing in my hand, so I answered it. 'Hello?' I said, half-hoping it was Benny. It wasn't. It was an aggressive voice asking to speak to 'Benjamin'. 'I'm sorry,' I explained, gently. 'Unfortunately, he's no longer with us.'

At that, the voice became abruptly enraged, demanding to know when he was going to get his fucking money.

'I don't know about your money, but if Benny's got it, you'd best come get it because he'll be six feet under soon.' Then I hung up, put the phone on silent and tucked it back in Benny's coffin.

I wonder about that call. From what I know of Benny, it's possible he took out a loan from some prick and used the funds to make his final year on earth one for the history books. Certainly, that's what I would do in his situation.

Sometimes life can challenge us, other times it can make us laugh. In my role as the Coffin Confessor I get the good, the bad, the funny and the sad, and each and every engagement is a pleasure. This one was particularly fun.

I've often asked those who have passed to send me a sign from the afterlife. If I ever received a sign from the other side this would have to have been it. A larrikin fucking with me from the great beyond by placing a call at the most awkward moment possible.

* * *

Benny died with the best kind of debt – the kind he'd never have to pay back. Then there was the opposite of that problem – dying with too much money and it making your final days a misery as the vultures circled.

Billy O'Connor was a surfer and hippie made good. He was a grommet who'd grown up surfing and smoking pot in Australia's newest international hotspot, Byron Bay. Once upon a time, Byron had been a sleepy beach town. These days it attracts the rich and famous, leaving many locals unable to afford to continue living in the breathtaking area of northern New South Wales. It's a haven for Hollywood celebrities and the carelessly wealthy. That wasn't Billy. He wasn't your average rich lister. In fact, he made his money not selling drugs or surfing but through screen printing. He had a passion for art and loved nothing more than to see his art on T-shirts, towels or togs. The customers loved it too, and he made a fortune out of his designs.

When he turned forty-five he decided to go to the doctors for a full physical. He thought it prudent to do this every five years. However good intentions are sometimes just that – intended – and the reality is Billy didn't get another physical until he was seventy-six. When he finally made it back to see the doc, he was diagnosed with aggressive prostate cancer. Removing it wouldn't help. The prognosis was not good. He was given less than twelve months to live, and it took him seven of those twelve to come to terms with the inevitable.

That wasn't helped by his family. He had an ex-wife and two adopted daughters who all became very attentive once they learned Billy's death was imminent. While his health declined, he thought for a while that he was surrounded by loved ones.

He soon began to see their intentions for what they really were. They were ostensibly providing the basic care he needed as death approached, but in reality, they were keeping close to make sure they stayed in the will. Worse than that, they were controlling his spending to make sure he didn't spend too much of his hard-earned money before he checked out.

Billy's ex-wife, who called herself Petal, never really left the 1960s. She acted, dressed and continued to believe she was part of the flower power culture long after it ended. She practised free love, which is a wonderful thing if everyone consents, except she never ran the idea by Billy while they were married. When he found out he was sharing his wife with other men, he decided this was not something he'd signed on for, and so they parted ways. However, Billy continued to support Petal and her two daughters – both fathered by other men, but who Billy raised as his own children.

After he got sick, Petal and her kids pretended to care for him on their terms, but Billy wasn't stupid. He'd been around long enough to know that Petal did not really care for him, and his children who'd lived too long in gentrified Byron had grown entitled. He knew people, family most of all, can become obsessed with money, especially when there's a chance of them getting their hands on it. But he also knew how to spend it and who needed it more.

In late 2021 he gave me a call. He was told about the Coffin Confessor by some colleagues and once he knew what I did he just couldn't stop thinking about it and had to reach out. He didn't want his funeral crashed. In fact, he didn't want a funeral at all. But he did want to put some things in place without his family, friends or colleagues knowing.

Material girl

He knew if he'd engaged his long-time lawyer then things would get messy. Same if he were to confide in a family member or close friend. So Billy thought it best not to disclose his intentions to anyone other than the one person he knew would do the job and have no vested interest in him. Of course that was me.

Once this was sorted, he quickly came to terms with his death sentence and set out to live life to the fullest. He went on a cruise, tried sky jumping, travelled to places he'd only read about and long wanted to visit. He spent time at the most luxurious resorts, eating and drinking whatever he wanted. Sometimes he over-indulged to the point that he'd be bedridden for a week, but that didn't stop him. He was determined to make the most of his time left among the living.

While Billy was living his best life, those closest to him were hoping his death would come sooner rather than later. They were concerned that he was spending his money on expensive and frivolous things such as trying to stay alive, while they had been carving up his estate and arguing over who would inherit what.

When the cancer worsened and he was confined to bed, he gathered his family together and told each of his dependents that he loved them dearly, and they would be very well looked after when he was gone. He was lying through his teeth but knew his ex and her children were gullible enough to believe him. So much so that he was very well looked after prior to his death.

Billy passed away in mid-2022, having spent a great deal of his fortune. He gave most of what was left to animal shelters, cancer research organisations, and his local lifesaving club. Only one major asset remained – his beloved screen printing business. This he left to a competitor that he'd nearly destroyed several times over the previous twenty years. Billy confessed to undercutting their quotes and stealing their staff but that he had a great respect and fondness for its director. Billy didn't think anyone in his inner circle could run his printing business. Giving it away to a rival would keep his workshop and craft alive, despite him being dead. His former rival gratefully received Billy's clientele, machinery, stock, contracts and warehouse.

The family was left very little. They tried to locate his will and/or the details contained in the will, but Billy's dying wish was that they be left out, and not be allowed to interfere with his donating his fortune to charity. Should they become upset or demanding then they could engage their own lawyer. If they do they'll find that Billy's last wishes are watertight and safe from even the slimiest estate lawyer's prying eyes. The Coffin Confessor saw to that.

* * *

Every so often I've had the privilege to help someone I genuinely liked. A handful of times, the bittersweet sadness of someone I loved.

My wife's family were always kinder to me than my own blood. That wouldn't be hard – my birth family fucking hates me, and the feeling is mutual – but Lara's went above and beyond to make me feel welcome, even when I wasn't all that great a prospect on paper. I got out of prison without a dollar to my name, no qualifications, and no assets, except for the love that Lara and I had for one another. I promised Marie, Lara's mother, that I would come good, and that no matter what, I would look after Lara whatever happened. That was enough for her.

Material girl

Good enough too for my wife's uncle Kevin. He was always a legend, and over the years we would often catch up for a beer and a chat. I don't particularly care for beer, but it was just a way of me letting him know I cared.

Kevin was thrilled to hear, see and read the stories of the Coffin Confessor. He would tell his mates and even people he just met all about his niece's husband. He was as stoked about my success as I was. Probably more so. But little did Kevin know that unfortunately he too would need my services, and sooner than he thought.

Kevin was in his eighties. He lived alone as his wife, Betty, was in a nursing home. She was unable to manage and couldn't remember who he was due to that fucking incurable disease – you know the one that makes you forget, the one called ... oh fuck it, I forget. Unfortunately, not too long ago Kevin also became ill and was transferred to palliative care. When he was taken to hospital, he texted me asking if I could come see him. I dropped everything and did as he'd asked. Parking at the hospital I noticed a nurse taking a quick photo of my car. This happens quite a lot. As a rule, people love muscle cars. They're nostalgic and bring back memories of the good old days.

As I headed to Kevin's room I could see some startled looks from some of the hospital staff. Since I've become known as the Coffin Confessor, hospital staff get a bit worried that I'm there to cause havoc on behalf of one of their patients. It's a shame. I have the highest regard for doctors, nurses and all hospital staff. They have the hardest job in the world. Luckily for them, I wasn't there to do mine that day, but to visit a loved one.

Once I reached Kevin's room I was surprised by how well he looked. But I knew he was about to ask me for a favour. He wanted me to go to his home and remove his safe, which he told me contained cash, papers and passports. Out of everything in the world, these were the possessions he most wanted to keep safe for his son, Dean. He asked that I look after the safe until Dean could return from where he was staying in Thailand. I promised Kevin that I would do it. I got onto Dean and organised for him to take receipt of the goods. Until I met him, all the items in the safe were secure and in very good hands.

I did, however, ask Kevin for a favour in return. He agreed without hesitation. In fact, after I told him my request, his face lit up and he gave a smile that seemed to last forever. I wasn't sure if it was due to the nature of the request or the fact that he was now holding the only unknown confession from the Coffin Confessor.

As soon as Dean flew back I handed over his father's safe. Both of us would continue to visit Kevin until his passing. His condition meant we couldn't share a beer, but I could still let him know I cared. The last time I visited Kevin, Dean sat on one side of his bed, and I sat on the other. We held Kevin's hands, telling him not to be afraid and that everything would be just fine.

Leaving that day, Kevin and I both knew it would be the last time we saw each other. But that's life. We live, we die, but it's what we do between the two that's important.

As I headed past reception I thanked the doctors and nurses for looking after Kevin. I wanted to show them my appreciation for the work that they do. They provide a service that's invaluable and they do it with all they have. It's a superhuman burden, while trying to juggle all the shit that comes with being a human being.

Material girl

Walking to my car, feeling sad in the knowledge I would never speak to Kevin again, I surprised a nurse who was taking a phone call. She seemed upset and was having a tearful argument with someone on her phone.

It was a bit of a reality check. I had the luxury to take time to feel sad walking out of the hospital, but ten minutes earlier this nurse had been calm and professional, providing strength to the sick and dying. In a few minutes' time, she would be back there again. But underneath that implacable, professional calm was a human being who might be falling apart. From a respectable distance, I gave her a quick smile and a nod, and got into my car.

Nurses, doctors, carers and all those who look after the children, the frail, the sick and the dying, have one thing in common: they have their own lives, their own problems, their own loves, likes and dislikes. For some fucking reason we often forget about this and treat them as though they are nothing but robots without feelings, cares or concerns. Of course, the reality is some come to work upset, lonely or tormented. Yet day in, day out, no matter how they're feeling, they always put yours first and foremost. Despite their own suffering. And despite dealing with the dead and dying every day.

As I say, in some ways I envy the dead. For one thing, their suffering is over. For another, they know what I don't. They've gone over into whatever-happens-next, and I'm deadly curious about that. So that's the favour I asked of Kevin. For him to go to wherever we go next and pass on a message for me. While holding his hand I looked him in the eyes and said, 'Mate, you're going before me and one day I will follow you but until then if there's a get-together in the afterlife can you please let Marie know that I turned out alright? I kept my promise and will continue to look after her little girl, Lara.'

Kevin grinned and nodded a sign he understood every word I'd said. With that I said my final goodbye.

*　*　*

Kevin checked out leaving very little baggage behind. Apart from some cash, some documents and some mementos he wanted his son to have, he wasn't weighed down by material possessions. The important things to him were the people in his life, his relationships and his memories. Which is a smart investment, because, let's face it, if you can take anything with you, that's probably going to be it.

The reality is, one moment you are here, the next you are gone, and chances are some relative or carer you hardly know is sifting through your shit, deciding what goes to charity and what they might make a buck out of on Gumtree. Most of the possessions you wasted your life working for will be thrown out. Some might find their way into a new home, but no one will love and care for them as much as you did. So why allow someone else to dispose of it all?

I was once engaged to retrieve some items from a client's home. When I arrived I discovered most of the household items had already been tossed into a large skip bin awaiting collection out front. The items included a large collection of books, wine glasses, trinkets and porcelain jugs collected from different places my client had travelled to. These were items that were once loved by their owner but now they were discarded.

I couldn't help but feel this is what my client's end of life had come to; no love, compassion or respect for what he'd valued. What a fucked way to go out.

I decided Kevin's option of travelling light was the way to go. I began to think about my own possessions and what they meant to me. Over the years I'd picked up a bunch of shiny toys – motorbikes, cars, mancave shit like that – which gave me a thrill for a bit, but after a while it's just more clutter. If I'm honest they meant very little to me. I made a resolution to start living with less emphasis on material things. To prove this to myself, I sold my beloved Ford XB Coupe. Although I kept the numberplates.

From there I decided to downsize and go through everything I own and 'Marie Kondo' the fuck out of it. I had to work out if a possession really meant something to me, or if it was just something else to worry about when I eventually dropped off the perch. It turns out that the majority of my shit was not something I would miss.

Selling, gifting or throwing away most of what I owned became a cathartic experience. I got to get rid of my shit, and all the stress that was attached to it over the years. Boy did it feel good. When I was done, the house was clean, my property was clear so the grass could grow, and there was plenty of room for visitors to park. Maybe too much room. And I did have a bit of spare cash after selling my muscle car.

So I replaced my bright-yellow XB Coupe with a bright-orange Mustang. Hey, I still need to get from A to B. I may as well do it in a ride that brightens up someone's day. People just love those new muscle cars. They remind them of the good old days.

5

Ash traveller

It was a miserable day in Grafton, in the middle of an unusually bitter winter for the Northern Rivers town, just over the Queensland border in New South Wales. In Maurice's family home, his relatives wore thick coats and jumpers against the cold while they sorted through his belongings. Maurice had recently gone into palliative care at the local hospital. He'd never be coming home. His next of kin had gathered to work out what to do with all his worldly possessions.

Technically, they weren't supposed to be there.

While they rifled through drawers and cupboards, arguing over what to do with his knick-knacks, they were trespassing, as the home was still Maurice's. Which meant they were all the more surprised when I walked in through the front door, nodded politely, walked to the fridge, pulled it out of its recess, lifted a floorboard, and took out a large camera case. I was walking out when one of the men retrieved his jaw from the floor and moved to stop me. 'Hang on,' he said. 'What the fuck are *you* doing?'

A fair question, but one that I could just as rightly ask of these people. They were surprised to see me and I was surprised to see them. This house – an old man's house with cardigans still hanging in the wardrobe and beer still in the fridge – was supposed to be empty. From a legal standing, we all had about as much right as each other to be there. Maurice's dearly beloved had gathered to ransack his shit and hunt for hidden treasures they knew were stashed somewhere. If it came down to it, and the police were called, as the family threatened to do, the law would come down on my side because I was the only one there with the homeowner's permission.

* * *

A few weeks earlier, having a beer at his local, Maurice had felt like he was in the prime of his life. Then suddenly he became nauseous and toppled over. The next thing he remembers was being rushed into an ambulance and taken to the nearest hospital. It would be weeks later that Maurice would be coherent enough to understand what had happened. The doctors told him he had an aneurysm and that he was very lucky to be alive at all. They also told him he should get his affairs in order soon. Which was great news as far as Maurice's children were concerned. He knew that the minute it was confirmed he was never going to see his home again his kids would start looting it.

Maurice didn't trust the banks. He kept his money in cash, hidden at home, along with certain private items that he wanted to stay private. He was in a bind – if on one hand he told his kids where he'd stashed his cash, they'd find his personal items too. He didn't want that. On the other hand, he could not rest easy without retrieving the items, as he knew his family would tear the house apart nail by nail to find the money. He had nowhere to turn, and confided this to one of his nurses, Bell. By chance, Bell had just seen me on TV and was reading my book. She called on Maurice's behalf shortly after that conversation.

* * *

It took some weeks to organise a meeting, and in that time, Maurice's death became not just likely but imminent. The morning I arranged to visit Maurice at the hospital was cold and wet. I'd travelled through Grafton a few times for work, but didn't remember it being so fucking cold. I make it a point of pride to ensure I'm fully prepared for a job – equipped with my body camera to gather evidence, legal documents, and any other tools I might need to complete my clients' requests. On this occasion, I'd forgotten to bring a fucking jacket and I shivered all the way from my car to the hospital cafeteria.

Once inside, the cold melted away pretty fast. That morning I appreciated the overheated air, while normally I couldn't stand it. I hate the way hospitals are overheated, which is unlucky for me, because my work takes me inside them regularly. When you do the maths, more people get worse in hospitals than get better, despite the best efforts of the medical staff. Every hospital has the same sense of death and stress about it. It's like they pump it through the ventilation ducts – along with the heat.

I took a seat in the cafeteria, where I'd arranged to meet Maurice's nurse, Bell. While I waited, I scanned the room. The staff were all lost in their own worlds – some picking at their food while scrolling, others scoffing it down as fast as they could between shifts. Their faces were determined, hopeful, worried. A few looked depressed and unwell. The gamut of human emotions, all crammed into this hot hospital café. I was lost in my own world, watching the carers absorbed in theirs when I felt a hand on my shoulder.

'Hi Bill, pleased to meet you. I'm Bell.' The voice belonged to a woman in her thirties wearing civilian clothes. She asked me if I'd like a coffee and said her shift started in twenty minutes, at which point she'd take me to meet Maurice. In the meantime, she ordered me a latte, reached into her bag, and pulled out a copy of my book. She placed it on the table and told me how much she'd enjoyed it.

This wasn't something I was used to while on a job, but I signed her book, and was happy to take a couple of quick selfies. By the time my coffee arrived, Bell had to run off to prepare for her shift. She was back not ten minutes later, dressed in the green scrubs of a palliative care nurse. Maurice was ready to see me.

Bell led me to the elevator and up to the palliative care ward. When we approached Maurice's room, she asked me to wait in the hall so she could check if Maurice was well enough to receive visitors. At that stage of palliative care, a patient can slip in and out of mental states quickly.

Maurice was perfectly lucid. He watched me closely as Bell placed a chair close to his bed for me to sit in, introduced us, and then took her leave. The first words out of his mouth were, 'Hey Bill, been speaking to any dead people lately?'

'Not lately, Maurice, but if you die on me while we're talking now you'll be the first!'

That put a smile on his face. In fact, he laughed so hard I think his catheter blew out. He then explained his situation and told me he'd hidden his most treasured possessions inside a combination lock-protected, hard-cased camera box. 'I want you to bring them to me.' He gave me a key to his front door and precise instructions on how to access his hiding spot, by prying up a floorboard underneath his fridge. I was to bring the camera case directly to him, but if he were to pass away before I made it back, then the case and its contents were to go to his grandson, Jason, who he was close with and trusted implicitly. What was in the case was for Maurice's eyes only. He was paying me to not be curious.

I told him that was all clear, and that his personal effects were none of my business. But I was curious about one thing. 'Why don't you just ask your grandson to collect your belongings if you trust him?'

'I don't want the family to turn on him,' he said. 'He's an honest boy and I don't want him to keep secrets for me. We need someone else so that Jason is kept separate and safe from judgement.'

'I understand completely,' I said, nodding. 'Is there anything else I need to know?'

'I can't pay you now, but there's cash inside the camera case, so you'll have to trust me.'

'That's fine, I trust you,' I told him. 'And if you think about taking the money and running, I know where to find you.' At this, Maurice gave another huge laugh. Bell came in to check if he was alright. He was still laughing as I left.

I went straight from the hospital to Maurice's house – a neat red-brick place in a row of similar houses in an unremarkable Grafton suburb. Very little jumped out at me. There was an unusual number of mid-range family cars on the street, but otherwise, there was nothing out of the ordinary. Certainly nothing to suggest the owner would never be coming home. I guess homes are like books – you can never judge them by their covers. You never know what goes on behind closed doors.

* * *

I wasn't expecting a crowd when I walked through the front door. The crowd wasn't expecting me either. The family – several generations of them – was scattered through the house, going through my client's belongings, pretty much ransacking the place like burglars. They turned towards me with a mix of astonishment and guilt on their faces. I made a split-second decision and decided to breeze through before they knew what was happening, then retrieved the camera case and headed back to the front door.

It was the right plan, because time would have given Maurice's family the balls to try to stop me. As it was, they didn't make a move until I was almost out the door, when one of the men tried to block me, standing in the doorway. That was a signal for the rest of the family to surround me. Like seagulls who have just seen one of their friends score a chip from a beach picnic, Maurice's family erupted into squawks of protest. None of them was game to lay a hand on me, but they were making a lot of noise about calling the police.

'Go ahead, call the police,' I said. This just seemed to confuse them. I had every right to come and go as I wished in my client's home and had a video contract to prove it, but that was a lot to explain to a responding officer in the heat of the moment. Best-case scenario, I'd have to show video evidence of Maurice engaging me on his behalf. Which would mean that they'd probably go and interview Maurice. Which is not something you want to burden a man with in his final hours.

Things were just coming to a head, and I was getting a bit annoyed at some of the more abrasive males in the group, when a young man stood up and sternly told everyone to calm down. This must have been Jason, the favoured grandson who was very close to his pop. I'm not sure how much he'd been told, but he spoke up and made the rest of the family understand that if I had a key, and knew the hiding place of the camera case without having to search for it, then I must be there on Maurice's request, and that we should respect that.

For my part, I admired that Jason had the guts to stand up for his grandfather and tell his family members to respect the dying man's wishes. To be honest, I was thankful for his assistance because dealing with the police is something I like to avoid. Call me superstitious, but I think it's bad luck when a cop crosses your path.

In the end, Jason came through so the family had to sit down and suck it up. The guy blocking the door moved away, I stepped down, and after thanking Jason for de-escalating the situation I drove straight to the hospital to give Maurice his camera case.

The old man's face lit up when he saw the case and he sat up in bed. After fumbling with the lock for a bit, he asked me to enter the combination for him. I did so and looked away while he opened the case. When I turned back he smiled a wide, happy grin at what he saw inside. He reached into the case, retrieved an envelope that was full of cash, and counted out our agreed amount. Then, with a contented sigh, he closed the case's lid, and with it, our business. With our affairs settled, I wished Maurice well. His days might have been numbered, but at least he had one family member looking out for him as the lid came down.

* * *

Jobs like this – sweeping homes for items at the request of the dying – quickly became one of the most common tasks people on their deathbeds asked me to perform. Everyone has embarrassing stuff hidden away. A few odds and ends that we quickly hide whenever visitors come by. Booze, drugs, porn, whatever guilty pleasure you enjoy in life, chances are it's still going to be there when you die. When people are hospitalised suddenly and realise that the walls of the palliative care ward might be the last they're ever going to see, those guilty pleasures become urgent liabilities.

For a surprising number of people who wait in death's green room for their curtain call, one of their highest priorities is having their homes swept for sensitive personal items. The thought of their grieving kids going through their possessions and finding a stash of vintage skin mags from the 1970s is unbearable for some old-timers. Or, like Maurice, they've got precious items stashed away that they want to make sure end up in the right hands. So they engage me to help out.

Removing sensitive items gives me an exclusive window into their lives. While it's far from embarrassing for me, I can understand my clients' hesitation when disclosing exactly what it is they want removed, returned or destroyed. Most have enough to deal with while they lay in wait for death to take them, and it's my job to assure them that discretion is paramount and that what they've requested me to do will be done, regardless of how potentially embarrassing their revelation might seem.

On one occasion I visited the unit of an elderly lady who engaged me to collect a few of her belongings and return them to her hospital bedside. When I arrived I found her sister going through the unit like a thief in the night. She was startled and confused as to why I was there and, predictably, threatened to call the police. I agreed and told her she could use my phone.

She did not take me up on the offer, and instead gathered what composure she had and left, yelling at me to stop recording her. I decline her request; it was in my client's best interest that she knew exactly what was going on. Luckily, the sister didn't uncover the items that were stored in the ceiling crawl space above the laundry, a place my client's departed husband had always said was safe. I guess he was right. In the ceiling was mainly cash – faded old $100 bills – but also a deeply personal, really quite sad item; a tiny jumpsuit, never worn, that was for meant for the stillborn baby the couple had had many years ago.

One man told me how his son found some sexual Polaroids of him and a woman he had been seeing for a few years after his wife had passed. A consensual sexual relationship between two adults, with no adultery involved, but the son was so grossed out that when he came to visit his father he threw the photos at him and screamed, 'You're a dirty fucking bastard and your death can't come fast enough!' By the time the old man hired me, it was too late to avoid that.

Another chap told me he confided in his son about the money he'd been saving, which he'd hid in his golf bag in his home. He told his son all this from his hospital bed. The son quickly left, went and grabbed the golf bag and the cash, and never came back. I was hired to track him down and recover the goods. I did so, but the man died without ever seeing his kid again.

I'm a line of last resort for all these people. The people who hire me for home sweeps have trust issues, are embarrassed and feel helpless. I happen to have the specific set of skills and the requisite amount of not-giving-a-fuck about protocol that allows me to help them with their specific needs.

From a legal standpoint, the way the law is written provides a clear window for me to operate in. As long as I have the permission of the homeowner to enter the premises and retrieve the items, then everything is above board. There's nothing illegal about picking a lock while breaking and entering a house. It's the breaking and entering that gets the law excited.

I've discussed my home sweeps with the police and while most are comfortable and understanding, there are exceptions. Police officers are people too, under the uniform, and they can be just as reasonable or pig-headed as anyone else. Some are real fucking creeps. I once had two officers say that they understood why I did home sweeps, because on a raid they loved nothing more than going through ladies' panty drawers and personal effects.

Now and again, I get calls from people who have heard about my home-sweep services and want me to go to a third party's home and retrieve items that belong to them. Take the woman who asked if it was possible for me to enter her ex-husband's home while he was being held by police for an unrelated matter and bring her items to compensate for child support he was avoiding paying. I had to explain to her, as gently as I could, that while she had my sympathies, I couldn't help her. What she was asking for – a home sweep *without* the permission of the homeowner – was a simple break and enter, and not something that I would be able to do. For that she would need a burglar, not a Coffin Confessor.

I've really grown to enjoy home sweeps. Not so much for the challenge – at this point I've got them down to a fine art – but for the window they provide into a stranger's world. I'm in the privileged position of getting to see another person's life up close and unfiltered, which is intriguing and surprising to say the least. I've been engaged to remove all types of items prior to family or friends getting their grubby little hands on them. But Grace, an elderly lady who'd had a fall, was the first who asked me to retrieve something with a first name.

'I want,' she told me shyly from her bed in the Royal Brisbane and Women's Hospital, 'for you to take care of Clive.'

* * *

Let's rewind a bit. Grace had lived in a government housing commission flat in the south-west of Brisbane. From a hard-up background, she'd worked her whole life as a nurse. After she retired from nursing, she decided that putting her feet up wasn't for her, so she did something completely different and got a job as a checkout chick at Coles. She should have been comfortable by this stage, but her husband left her after twenty-seven years of marriage for his secretary and the shock of the betrayal, and the divorce, took its toll on all facets of her life. None more so than her finances and her health. They're two things most if not all of us can't live without. In the blink of an eye, Grace went from having a car, career, husband and home to living in a housing commission flat. Then she had a fall, and even living at home was no longer a possibility.

Grace's daughter contacted me on her mother's behalf. She lived in Adelaide, too far away to drop everything and rush to help her mother with her hospitalisation. Grace's daughter asked about my home-sweep services and whether I could find a way into Grace's home in order to retrieve a few essential items. These were to be delivered to Grace's bedside to make her time in hospital a little more comfortable. I was given the address and told where I could find a spare key hidden in the letterbox.

Once I arrived at the block of flats I could immediately tell they housed some of the less fortunate in our society. Grace's flat was a bit like where I lived as a kid – the same cheap brickwork and baking concrete yards of government housing. I opened Grace's letterbox, reached inside and felt around until I located a key wrapped in Blu tack stuck to the roof of the letterbox. While I was removing the Blu tack from the key, an elderly lady walked past, watching my every move. I ignored her. When it comes to nosy neighbours, any attempt to ingratiate or explain myself only increases the likelihood of them calling the cops. In 90 per cent of situations, simply carrying yourself with the courage of your convictions is enough to discourage anyone thinking of being a nuisance.

Undeterred, I made my way to Grace's apartment, entered, and closed the door behind me. My instructions were to collect Grace's computer, iPad and a large wallet containing a number of documents, as well as her reading glasses, a handbag and any money left behind. However, all I could find was the computer, the document wallet and the iPad – this last item hidden in the back of a cupboard. While searching for the other bits and pieces, I opened a bedside drawer and found a large sex toy. It was unlikely Grace's reading glasses were hiding under that, so I closed the drawer and took my leave.

I then returned to the hospital. Grace's daughter had given me her mother's ward and bed number and as I peeked into Grace's room I could see she was awake. I entered and just as I was about to introduce myself, Grace told me that her daughter had called and told her to expect me. As I placed the items on a chair close to Grace's bed she asked if it were possible for me to do one last thing for her.

'Of course,' I said. It would be a really sick bastard who would say no to a dying woman. 'How can I help?'

She told me that she wanted me to find 'Clive' and take care of him. Grace had the deathly pale colour that people at the very end of their life often take on, but as she explained who Clive was, some colour returned to her cheeks.

Clive was her sexual partner. Her *only* sexual partner since her husband started fucking his secretary. 'The affair only lasted eight months before she left him,' she told me with some satisfaction. It was the only thing that seemed to make her smile. Clive, on the other hand, had been loyal and tended to her night after night without fail. Provided she remembered to change his batteries.

Clive, of course, was the sex toy I'd glimpsed while sweeping Grace's home. It had given her so much happiness and comfort in the wake of her divorce that she'd come to consider it a good friend, and christened it Clive, so that he could have a personality of his own. But now she was very embarrassed. She was mortified at the thought of her daughter finding Clive – to the point where she was turning to me to help. I offered to go back to her flat, retrieve Clive, and give him a proper Viking funeral. I destroyed Clive in the incinerator at the back of my property where I destroy all my clients' sensitive items. Then I sent the video to Grace to watch on her iPad.

As I'd left Grace's hospital room a few days earlier, I knew it would be the first and last time I'd ever see her. I'm glad I did though. It costs nothing to be kind, especially to a nice old lady that the world has fucked over. I helped her in a way no one else in her life could have, and while I wasn't there when she received the video, I hope that as she watched her final request play out, Clive put a smile on her face, one last time.

* * *

Helping the dying settle their worldly affairs against the express wishes of unkind family members has become a frequent request. Most commonly, like the stories above, I'm hired to save someone from embarrassment, or to preserve a beloved object. But then there's a third option, something I do for those who see death coming over the horizon only to recognise they have been abandoned by their family, and who choose to celebrate their independence in style.

I've witnessed otherwise loving family members letting go of their loved one before they're even in the ground. While this sounds terrible it's just their way of coping, but for those who are knocking on death's door it's heartbreaking.

At what point do we let someone go? On their deathbed? At their funeral? Days, weeks, months, even years after their death? Or even years *before*, when an elderly person becomes inconvenient to the busy, modern life of the young. In my experience, there's no set rules on letting go. It doesn't mean letting go of the love or hate you had for them, it just means it's time for you to move on.

In Annie Packer's case, this was quite literally what happened.

Annie was a 72-year-old widow with three daughters and five grandchildren. She'd been a widow most of her life – she'd married her beloved, Bart, at the age of twenty-two, and just six years later was widowed when he died in a motorcycle accident. Since then, Annie had lived a simple life of sacrifice, working to provide for her family. And she wouldn't let Bart go. She never married again or even dated another man; she truly lived for her children and grandchildren, doing everything for them until they were old enough to get on with their own lives. At this point, they effectively abandoned her. Annie was left all alone. Even her daughters stopped visiting as their need for their mother's babysitting duties had all but vanished.

The struggle of loneliness is real and is endemic in our society. It's particularly brutal for the elderly as the support networks they've created for others in their lives are abandoned. It causes all types of mental health issues and shortens lifespans considerably. It's easy enough to give a lonely person platitudes, 'Join a club, go for a walk, move into a retirement community!' Like moving into a fucking community of retirees all suffering loneliness and depression is going to help. That'd be like trying to cure alcoholism by switching from wine to whiskey.

Personally, I embrace my own company. Sure, I'm surrounded by loved ones, but even then you can still feel alone. While it may be a struggle for most it's not for me; I people watch and after an hour or two of observation I'm very happy to be left alone. It's my therapy, so to speak.

But Annie was bitter that she'd been abandoned by her family. She became angry and upset at being dumped like a dog on the side of a highway hoping someone will come along and take care of her. She looked at her situation realistically – she knew that single women over fifty were invisible, and if her family had ghosted her, they weren't coming back.

Annie didn't want revenge, but she didn't want to wither away and die of loneliness. She called me, because she knew I dealt with the dead and dying. She realised she needed to understand what she had to put in place now rather than later, especially should her children decide to become her power of attorney and force her into aged care.

When I first met Annie she looked old and unkempt, not at all what her polite, polished voice and demeanour over the phone had led me to expect. It was clear that she was suffering badly from isolation, even if her physical health was still reasonably good. Her home on the other hand was well kept and very clean. On the cabinet that sat beneath the television, hung an urn.

'Is that your husband Bart's resting place?' I asked gently.

She acknowledged it was, invited me to sit for tea, and for close to an hour I listened to Annie talk about her daughters and grandchildren. They'd treated her shabbily, but not a bad word was spoken about any of them. I could tell that she loved her family and was in a world of pain and needed some guidance.

As the Coffin Confessor with all the powers of a private investigator, there was little I could do but arrange for her to engage a lawyer and have her will changed – putting something in place that would stop her daughters seeking power of attorney. With all that in mind, I declined her offer of hiring the Coffin Confessor. If she had hired me, that was the most I could do. But I could sit here, not as the man who crashes funerals, but as someone who could take the time to listen, really listen, to a lonely older lady. We began to talk in a way I don't think anyone had done with Annie for a long time.

During our conversation, she told me she had a bit of money and quite a lot of equity in her home.

'You could take the equity here, get off your arse, grab Bart and go explore this great country we live in,' I said. I suggested that she could rent out her home for a good price, take out a loan and buy a campervan – one big and comfortable enough for a grey nomad like her. After looking at her finances I told her that the rent would cover her loan, petrol, insurance and incidentals, plus give her a bit of savings, something she was very happy to hear. As we spoke I could see her face light up, I could feel her energy and enthusiasm return.

When I left I knew I had planted a seed. Sometimes that's all that's needed. I knew Annie would be fine. I also knew it wouldn't be the last time I heard from her.

Sure enough, it wasn't long until I got the call asking if I could take a look at a campervan she had found on the internet. While doing her research, she had started planning the itinerary for a trip of a lifetime – and would record her travels, which she would post on her Facebook page. She told me about the campervan and it was more than adequate. It wasn't huge, but big enough and comfortable enough, with a kitchen, a shower, a toilet and a queen-size bed. I inspected the van, impressed at the bargain she got, and suggested she should get a mechanic to go over it, but I did give her my thumbs up.

'It's perfect for you,' I said.

'Perfect for me,' she replied, showing me the passenger seat where Bart would ride shotgun. 'And for my husband.'

She said she would keep in touch, and true to her word, soon enough she reached out again. Just nine weeks since I first met Annie and four weeks since viewing the campervan I got a call. Annie was excited to tell me that she had all of her possessions in storage and was getting far more rent than expected for her home. She was phoning from the road. She and Bart were already on their big trip, not far from the beautiful seaside town of Coffs Harbour, the place she and Bart visited just after they were married.

Annie also confessed that she hadn't told her daughters yet and said her first post would come as a shock to them. This was something I was delighted to hear. She thanked me for giving her some quality of life but to be honest all I did was encourage her to do something I believe she had been thinking of doing all along.

Sometimes, all a person needs to make a life-changing decision is for someone to provide the spark. That's one service the

Coffin Confessor provides for free. Then again, once or twice, it's been a two-way street, and meeting Mike Megan gave me an idea to make my own life better.

* * *

Mike Megan was also a traveller. In life there was nothing he loved more than exploring the open road and seeing where it took him. In death, he wanted more of the same. He called me, asking about the Coffin Confessor services on offer. He had a specific request in mind for his remains. One I thought was very interesting. Mike wanted his ashes placed into a small urn and posted to a random address in Germany – a country he had travelled extensively through and had always wanted to see again.

The urn would be engraved with instructions asking whoever possessed it to take it with them on their next trip, and then pass it on to another traveller at the new destination. The hope was that whoever found his remains would take him on the journey, and then pass him along to another traveller. This way, Mike and his ashes could keep on travelling via the good intentions of fellow travellers, theoretically forever.

It was a fascinating idea, and easy enough to do. The tricky part would be coming up with the right wording so that the receiver knew exactly what was in the urn and what to do with it if they were up for the adventure. Mike and I went back and forth for a while on the instructions, but at a certain point he changed his mind and cancelled his request.

No worries, that happens from time to time – although the more I thought about the concept, the more it grew on me.

The Ash Traveller. It had a nice ring to it. It was a great idea and triggered something within me that gave me the opportunity to finally do what I'd been putting off for decades.

* * *

My father's ashes sat in my garage for over thirty years. It's not that I couldn't decide what to do with them – it was just that sometimes I forgot they were there for long stretches at a time. Other times, I'd go into the garage to grab a tool, come across the ashes, and in some ways they made me feel connected to a man I didn't really know, but loved in my own way.

I barely knew my father. He left when I was very young, about four years old, and I always regretted not meeting him. While I was surviving childhood, and the physical, sexual and emotional abuse of my so-called caregivers, I used to fantasise about my dad coming back to rescue me. But he never did, and some say that might have been for the best, given he was a gangster, a murderer and a thug. Nonetheless, I still believe it would have been a meet and greet both he and I would never have forgotten.

The closest I ever got to a tangible, actual connection with my dad was when I was in solitary confinement in Boggo Road Gaol and met a prison guard who had fond memories of him. The guard told me my dad had been locked in the adjacent cell, and that he was one of the most feared men in Boggo Road. Even then, even into adulthood, I had an idealised idea of the man, and what it meant I could be. And I loved him for that.

* * *

Billy Edgar was known in the underworld as the Irishman. Throughout the 1960s and 70s, he worked in pubs and clubs from Melbourne to Sydney's notorious Kings Cross – places like the infamous Pink Pussy Cat and Les Girls – eventually becoming a bodyguard for entertainers Frank Sinatra, Bob Hope and countless others.

Another of his jobs was collecting money from various nightclub bosses. On one occasion, he was asked to drive to the Gold Coast to confront the owner of the Surfers Paradise Beer Garden and demand a payment with the offer of protection. However, what he didn't know was the Beer Garden was already paying for protection – and it wasn't to gangsters from Sydney or Melbourne but detectives from Brisbane and the Gold Coast. It was a police trap, and Dad walked right into it. The Irishman was arrested and thrown into a cell not far from the one the son he'd left behind would inhabit years later.

Legends about Billy the Irishman still pop up quite frequently. He was implicated in the 1973 firebombing of Brisbane nightclub the Whiskey Au Go Go, which resulted in fifteen people losing their lives. That was part of an ongoing war between local Brisbane operators and gangsters from the southern states making moves. It's also alleged my dad was ordered to attend meetings in Melbourne's Little Italy on Lygon Street, which back then was a mobsters' playground. Rumour has it he was sent to collect cash from businesses that were reluctant to pay their protection money. He became an integral part of the Italian underworld, despite his strong Irish accent and stature. He was a legend in Melbourne, but ironically it was that trip to the Gold Coast that would see him arrested and jailed for extortion.

The life and legend of my dad are on the public record for anyone who knows where to look, and now and again I'll get a call from a true crime podcast reporter who's done his homework and wants to fact-check a thing or two. I'm always happy to help. I've enjoyed having this connection to the dad I never really knew, but who I had a relationship with, if only in my head and in the memories echoing through the prison bars.

My father didn't teach me to be a man. But neither did any of the other men in my life. My mother surrounded herself with sick and twisted blokes, so she didn't have a clue what a good man was. She was blinded by the love for her violent, wayward husband and her perverted father – my grandfather and abuser. In the end, the only one who taught me how to be a good man was a little boy, a kid named Joshua, my only son. Seeing him as a baby, through the window of a visiting box in prison and not being able to reach out and hold him because I'd fucked up and gotten myself locked up, was one of the most heartbreaking feelings you can imagine.

That was the start of a long road for me – stepping out of my father's footsteps, which had led me to prison, and walking my own path. It took the love of my son, and my daughter, Candis, to teach me how to do that. Their love – and now that of their children, my grandchildren – continues to make me a better man.

The family I've created with Lara is far more important than the family I come from, if you could call them family. I have a younger brother who doesn't know if he's straight, bi or gay and it's of no concern to me. Once in a while his offspring come knocking on my door asking me to help them understand their father, and I can only tell them what I know and it isn't much. I have a younger sister who hates the world who only appeared in my life when she thought she might make some money selling stories about me. I've also got an older sister I know nothing about.

And let's not forget a mother I wouldn't wish on my worst enemy. I'm not afraid to call a spade a spade, and my mother was a 24-carat cunt. My American friends are appalled when I say that to them. 'How can you call your mother that word?'

To which I say, 'If you ever met her, you would agree.'

But I don't give the people and places that I come from any headspace. This has allowed me to move on from life as 'a survivor'. I'm no longer a victim of the circumstances that tormented me as a child. That meant becoming a better person – one my kids could count on, and have happy memories of, not just war stories from prison guards told as part of an endless cycle of abuse.

My father was everything I refused to be but little did I know just how alike we were. We both fought, struggled and were imprisoned, both worked for nightclub bosses and those needing tasks done that others were too afraid to do. The apple didn't fall far from the tree in some respects. But a tree can grow much, much bigger than the shadow it starts under. For me, the traits I took from my father were the fact that no matter what happened, I wanted to be me. No false, fake, pretentious bullshit. Just me being me. I kept the individuality that Billy the Irishman had, and discarded the bullshit.

When he died, I ended up inheriting his ashes, and without any great inspiration on what to do with them, I put them in the garage and out of mind until Mike's idea gave me some inspiration. After a lot of thought and consideration it was finally time to set my father's ashes free. From everything I knew of him, I decided an urn wasn't his style. Billy the Irishman would have appreciated a good whiskey feast.

I placed his ashes into four small metal flasks of the type that old men and teenagers smuggle into social events to take a swig from. The flasks needed to be engraved and I came up with the perfect script that would have those who found him either pass him on or leave him for someone else to find.

> *My Dying Wish*
> *Help Me Travel The World*
> *If You're In Possession Of My Ashes*
> *Please Leave Me*
> *On A Bus, Train or Plane*
> *And Let The Next To Find Me*
> *Do The Same*
> *Thank You*
> *Ash Traveller*

Once the flasks were ready I posted them off to begin travelling the world. One went to a hotel called Some Random Bar in Seattle. One to the Narrow Bar in Vancouver. One was left on a platform at London Bridge train station by a colleague who had business there and agreed to help out. The last was sent to the Grand Central Hotel in Belfast. Unfortunately, the flask meant for Some Random Bar (that I'd chosen by random) never made it to its destination. The United States has some of the most tight-arsed border controls on the planet, and Seattle rejected my father's ashes and sent his Irish arse back to my post office box. So that meant it was on to plan B.

Shortly afterwards, while travelling to northern New South Wales to visit my son, I called into a roadhouse. It was one of those big petrol stations set up to fuel trucks carrying goods across the country. A bank of restaurants, the obligatory McDonald's or KFC or, if you're lucky, a roadhouse-style café with a bain-marie full of homemade food and a counter that serves the worst coffee on the planet.

These roadhouses allow truckers to rest, take a shower, have a feed and a bit of a chat in between shifts behind the wheel. As I pulled in, I could see the diner lit up like an aquarium, the truck drivers sitting in booths, either socialising over a cuppa or alone and hunched over their dinner plates. Outside, in the dark, their big rigs lined up at rest, waiting for their owners to return.

I filled up and went into the petrol station, where I made some small talk with a few of the drivers. One of them pointed out his big blue rig, which he was about to drive over 4000 kilometres to Western Australia. I chose to put my father's ashes in the care of this driver. I don't know if my old man ever got a chance to see Western Australia and the great western deserts while he was alive. But he would now. The only issue was the driver had no idea he had an extra passenger as I'd placed my father's ashes in a secure part of the truck invisible to prying eyes.

Every person on this planet is going to die and every person will either be buried or cremated, yet very few will continue the journey. Some know they'll be buried close to a loved one or in their local cemetery while others don't care where their ashes end up.

I, for one, know I'll be spread over the ocean and not stuck on a fucking shelf, in a box or placed underground. Unless my final wishes aren't granted, which makes me think I might need a Coffin Confessor, as so many have done before.

6

Till death do us part

When news about an Australian man crashing funerals first went viral, I received many, many requests for interventions at the end of life. One of them sparked my curiosity, partly because of the discreet way I was approached. One afternoon, my phone rang and a man identified himself as a medical doctor. He was dying, literally, but he also had a secret that was killing him and a confession he needed to make. I agreed to meet him anonymously at a café on the Gold Coast.

I had a hunch that I knew who this anonymous medic was. Long before I became the Coffin Confessor, back when I was a PI, I'd been hired by a stripper named Carry to look into the behaviour of a certain Gold Coast doctor who she claimed was drugging her, holding her against her will, and sexually assaulting her. The investigation had me frequenting strip clubs, brothels and the one place I knew better than most, the streets.

I'd given the target of my investigation the nickname 'Dr Feelgood' after my first night of inquiries, and not because he seemed to be particularly good at his job. I never saw him practising much actual medicine; he seemed to spend more time in establishments that sold sex and lap dances. However, every young woman that he came into contact with seemed to be in a much better mood after they'd spent time alone with him.

Dr Feelgood lived in a luxurious apartment complex in a prominent Gold Coast suburb. Staking out his pad and gaining access wasn't going to be easy, especially if I had to record his exploits for future evidence. At least, it should have been a challenge, but Dr Feelgood made it a cinch. He was a creature of habit, every day the same routine: dinner, a few drinks, a visit to a particular strip club, splash the cash, and take home a young, beautiful girl or two. Girls he must have thought loved and adored him. Fucking idiot.

It wasn't hard to work out what they were getting from the relationship. I doubted Dr Feelgood was some sort of stud in the bedroom brightening these jaded working girls' night with romance. And he definitely wasn't a strapping young buck; he was older, overweight, tired and a bit saggy. He dressed rather well, but a nice outfit only goes so far, particularly if it's left on the floor of a Gold Coast brothel. By the end of my investigation, it was my professional opinion that the thing that made Dr Feelgood so popular was his liberal use of his right to prescribe drugs. Several sources confirmed drugs, scripts, and young girls being lured by opioids to sex parties. I now knew why the young women I'd seen were happier after meeting Dr Feelgood.

While following him around, from strip club to café to casino then back to strip club again, I never witnessed him meeting with anybody of suspicion – no drug kingpin or street operator, just the working girls he seemed to favour. He appeared at home and comfortable moving through the sometimes hectic streets. Not a care in the world.

However, on one occasion, while leaving a club in Surfers Paradise, Dr Feelgood was approached by two young men who I suspected were looking for an easy target to roll for a buck. Someone who dressed well, wore a watch and gold jewellery, flashed the latest model of mobile phone – but most importantly was old and vulnerable. Dr Feelgood was what you'd class as an easy target. A horny old man stumbling out of a strip club dripping with gold and cash was *exactly* the sort of mark I'd look for back when I was a kid on the street.

I was sure that Dr Feelgood was about to get mugged, but then two heavily built doormen came down from the club and escorted him to a waiting limousine. They opened the door for him and shook his hand, allowing for a transfer of a small item. I snapped all of this with my long-lens camera, but couldn't see whether he was handing over drugs, or just a cash tip to the doormen for their kindness. It was clear that Dr Feelgood had minders. These strip club bouncers lived in the grey area between regular sleaze and organised crime, and if they were allied with the doc, he was more than just your average patron getting his rocks off.

One of the first things I do when I'm engaged to investigate anything related to a crime – be it money laundering, drugs, or a domestic – is contact the local detectives and let them know what I'm up to. I do this regardless of them giving a fuck or not. That way I make sure it's on the record. If the shit hits the fan none of it lands on me. I knew this was a criminal matter, but I had everything I needed for my investigation.

After a few weeks of following Dr Feelgood I received a call from an investigative journalist mate asking what I was working on. When I told him about the doc and his exploits his ears pricked up. 'Do you think there's a story in it?'

'It's a doctor on the Gold Coast buying sex, snorting cocaine and selling scripts,' I said. 'Yeah, I think there's a story in it.' But I asked him not to do anything rash until I had a few days to compile my report and send it to the police. He agreed.

After handing my investigation over to the detectives my job was done. Now it was their investigation. I'd done all I could, and it was up to the cops to do with it what they may. From there, it went to the medical board, but that wasn't my concern.

That's the best thing about being a private investigator: you follow people, observe them, get to know them, write a report, take a few pics, or record an event, then hand over the material. You walk away and don't give a fuck about the outcome. It's like being a wildlife scientist of the urban jungle – I do my job and then fuck off without disturbing the delicate balance of scumbags making their way in the ecosystem.

So I hadn't given the matter much thought for years. But when I got a call from a Gold Coast doctor with a guilty conscience, I assumed I was about to be reunited with my old mate Dr Feelgood.

* * *

It turned out I was wrong! The man waiting for me in the café was a total stranger. Like Dr Feelgood, he was also of an advanced age, but there the similarities ended. He dressed well, but in muted, professional clothes, not the flashy kit of a Gold Coast gangster's associate. A doctor, yes, but a Good Doctor. Well respected in his field, hardworking and compassionate. But he had a secret that was weighing heavily on him that he wanted to confess.

'It's a secret that most doctors have, but while it's an open secret for us in the field, it's rarely discussed. Can I trust you?'

'Anything you tell me stays with me unless it's a confession to a crime of a serious nature,' I explained. 'If you've harmed somebody, and are at risk of harming someone else, I'm obliged to tell the authorities. For example, if you tell me you've committed a murder, I'd have to call the cops right now.'

What he confessed was not a crime like murder. But it was borderline, to say the least. The Good Doctor said he'd been administering lethal doses of morphine to patients in end-of-life care. The sick and elderly who were already knocking on death's door or those he knew without a shadow of a doubt were not going to pull through. He did this as a last resort to spare the terminally ill the worst of their suffering before the inevitable happened. He also told me that when he was a young practitioner in his home country, where resources were scarce and life was cheap, he was introduced to the practice not for care or compassion reasons but to free up space within the healthcare system. To be honest, I wasn't quite sure if the Good Doctor was a saint or a sinner.

I couldn't help being blunt. 'Okay, but why am I here, doc? I feel like this is one for the confessional booth. I can't offer you support or resolution for what you've done.'

My bluntness worked. He wanted me to deliver an afterlife gift to a man named Mitch. It turned out the doctor had given

Mitch's wife, Beth, a lethal dose of morphine in order to end her suffering. Before Beth died she asked that her one remaining precious possession, a gold necklace, be given to her husband after she was gone. For some reason, years later, the memory of Beth still haunted the doctor. He didn't tell me exactly what it was about her death that had shaken him to the core, but she was the last person he ever euthanised. He was still losing sleep over it and was looking for some sort of resolution. Truth be told, I think his own mortality had spurred him on to finally calling me.

After he'd administered the morphine that killed Beth, he'd taken the necklace from her body so that it wouldn't be lost as sometimes happens en route to the morgue. People who commit some of the most heinous crimes often keep mementos – a lock of hair, some clothing, or a piece of jewellery. So this was a red flag for me, but the doctor had a reasonable explanation. He insisted that he had never taken anything from his deceased patients, except for this one time. He'd intended to return the necklace to Mitch after Beth died, but he'd never found the courage to do so. That's what he needed me for. To deliver a gift to Mitch, from Beth in the afterlife.

* * *

Tracking down Mitch wasn't hard as the doctor had me given his address and personal details. With the gold necklace in hand I began my journey. It was in the late evening by the time I arrived at the home that Mitch had shared with his late wife. The front door was wide open, and from there I could see through to the kitchen where a young lady was preparing a meal. She was wearing nothing but a long white T-shirt that barely covered her arse. Before I could get her attention, a man who I assumed was Mitch came to the door and in an angry and confronting tone asked who I was and what I wanted.

This is the usual response when I do a face-to-face. Responding with an even angrier and more confronting reply normally short-circuits the mouthy blokes and sees me hold the upper hand.

'I'm the fucking Coffin Confessor,' I barked in the bloke's face. 'And I've got a gift from Beth.'

Mitch simmered down quickly, and I explained who I was and why I was standing at his front door. I'd expected the initial aggro, but I also expected some emotion once he understood why I was there. Sadness, or gratitude, or even more anger. Something. Anything. But he just appeared distracted and bored. He didn't seem to care about his dead wife's final gift. He seemed more interested in getting back to the young, scantily dressed brunette now sitting on his dining-room table, legs stretched out provocatively, drinking white wine.

I understood then that the necklace, and by extension his wife's memory, meant fuck all to Mitch. I imagined him taking it and giving it to the young lady lounging in the dead woman's house. I thought then about just telling him some bullshit story and not handing over Beth's necklace, but I'm engaged to do a job no matter how confronting or unethical it may be. So I gave Mitch Beth's gold necklace and left without saying anything more.

I had a bad taste in my mouth, but it is what it is. It's not my job to judge Mitch for seemingly moving on so fast. At the end of the day, even if he never thinks about Beth, then at least she lives on in the thoughts, and maybe nightmares, of the Good Doctor. The one man who actually gave enough of a shit to provide peace and closure to a dying woman.

After my meeting with the Good Doctor I took it upon myself to investigate and explore what he had done in more detail. The more I did the more it became apparent that the practice was widely known and not discussed. Doctors even have a name for it – acting as the 'Angel of Death', otherwise known as assisted voluntary euthanasia. In most states in Australia, up until the end of 2023, assisting with euthanasia has been illegal. Until very recently, the law stated that if somebody is at the end of life, or in a vegetative state with no hope of recovery, then actively ending their life in an act of mercy meant breaking the law. The best practice in end-of-life care was to pump a patient full of opiates and dissociative drugs and wait for them to starve to death or die of dehydration. It's fucking barbaric. A traumatic way to die for both the deceased and their loved ones who had to watch.

I get occasional requests from sick people who are suffering to help them end their time on earth. It's heartbreaking, but I have to tell them I can't, even though I think it's the moral thing to do. Could I? Absolutely, in a heartbeat. Would I? Probably not. I wouldn't tell anybody if I did. But still, the requests keep coming. Sometimes in the strangest of places.

* * *

It was a cool and blustery Tuesday morning on the Gold Coast Broadwater. I'd ventured out for a walk first thing to start the day on the right foot. This is something I've been doing for many years – forty minutes one way and then back. But this morning's walk would be different.

When I got back to the car park I saw two elderly people embracing. They were staring not at the spectacular water views but into each other's eyes, with an intensity that suggested they could not stand to look away from each other for long, let alone be separated. I smiled and felt I was witnessing the sort of love my wife Lara and I have for each other. As I walked past the couple the lady returned my smile.

'Good morning,' said the gentleman.

'Good morning,' I replied, and kept walking.

As I got to my car, the lady piped up, 'Excuse me. Do you mind if I ask what your number plates mean?' She was referring to my COFNFSR custom plates.

'That's my job title,' I told her. 'I'm the Coffin Confessor.'

This brought a puzzled look to her face, but the gentleman must have recognised the name and turned to his wife excitedly. 'This is the guy I was telling you about.' He went on to explain that he'd seen me on TV.

I was taken aback for a moment trying to think which TV show it was. At that point, I'd done so many that I'd lost track.

'I'm Antonio, and this is my wife, Jules,' the man then said. 'If you're not in a hurry, could you please tell my wife about what you do?'

I wasn't in a rush and was happy to explain. The couple listened, paying close attention and without interrupting me, but as I spoke, they shared a sly smile. I felt compelled to ask what was on their mind.

Jules explained that she and Antonio had been together for over sixty years but, now in old age, they feared being separated if they were forced into aged care. They had a toxic relationship with their only son. His priority seemed to be getting his hands on their home and assets, even if it meant having them consigned to aged care against their explicit wishes.

The fear of going into a nursing home to benefit an ungrateful next of kin wasn't new to me. Nor was it uncommon. I'd spoken with a lot of people over the years about the predators waiting like funnel-web spiders in the family for their moment to bite. But Antonio and Jules's idea for a solution was something else. They'd decided to make a radical decision so they'd never be apart again. Still with a mischievous look on their faces, they shared what they wanted to do, and asked if I could help. I admit, for once in my life, I was speechless.

Jules asked if we could meet the following week to discuss things in more detail. She gave me Antonio's mobile number and their address, and I agreed to meet them on Friday morning 10 a.m. Antonio asked me to keep their conversation under wraps as he feared if word got out they would be dragged into aged care or worse – sectioned for mental health reasons, medicated, and separated. I gave them my word that nothing they said would be repeated.

* * *

That week flew by. In fairness, most weeks fly by now that I'm over fifty. Time just seems to go faster and faster every day. I'm not sure why. Maybe it's because there are fewer miles left on the road and the landscape goes by quicker. Maybe Father Time is just a hoon and a rev-head and puts his foot on the gas as you get past city limits.

But before I knew it, it was Friday morning, and I was pulling into the driveway of Antonio and Jules's residence, a small house perched on a very large block of land with beautiful gardens and flower beds that would have any proud gardener green with envy.

I was walking towards the front door when I heard Jules yell out, 'We're round the back! Come on through!' So I made my way through the gardens to a backyard that boasted the most beautifully manicured lawn I'd ever seen.

'My pride and joy,' Antonio nodded when he saw me admiring the lawn. 'This is where we want the magic to happen.'

'Please,' Jules said, gesturing towards a small, tasteful outdoor furniture set-up, which was laid out with a pot of tea and biscuits. 'Make yourself at home.'

After a sip of tea and a Tim Tam, Antonio explained in more detail what it was they wanted from me, elaborating on the plan they'd confided in me a week earlier. In short, he and Jules wanted to end their lives on their own terms. They'd devised a meticulous plan on how they would do it painlessly, in each other's arms. When they'd first told me about it back at the Gold Coast Broadwater, I worried that I was hearing a confession of intent of a murder–suicide. Now, as they walked me through their plan, I understood that this wasn't some salacious true crime story. It was a true *love* story.

Antonio said he didn't need my help with them taking their own lives. This was a great relief as the thought had crossed my mind several times since we first met. He asked instead that

I carry out a few of their wishes once I became aware of their deaths. I didn't have a problem with this. That's my job. In this case, it would be an honour. The couple wanted their ashes collected after their cremation and secretly spread among their flower beds. Antonio wanted some thrown over his beautifully manicured lawn as well – so that he could continue tending to it and helping it grow after his passing. After these tasks were done, and it was too late to intervene, I was to approach their son and deliver a letter they'd co-written that would explain why they'd done what they'd done and ask for his understanding. A will was already in place that dictated how their assets and belongings would be distributed. Antonio and Jules wanted me to keep an eye on the legal proceedings, and make sure the will was actioned uncontested.

While I sat and listened, I interjected several times. I asked if they needed help or counselling. I even tried to offer them an alternative to their fear of having their autonomy taken away. But I soon gave up. I could see it was pointless by the look in their eyes. They knew exactly what they wanted and what they were intending to do.

Truthfully, I couldn't argue with their logic. They told me some horrible stories of abuse within the aged care system. Over the past ten years, they'd lost a number of friends who'd suffered and died miserably after being dragged against their will into nursing homes. A good friend was forced to wear a nappy – she was not incontinent – but due to staff shortages it was easier for them to let her defecate on herself than help her use the toilet. From sitting in her own filth for hours at a time, she succumbed to sores that became infected and ultimately hastened an excruciating death. Another friend was refused visitors because he'd become outspoken and would beg to be released from imprisonment. The staff, wary of causing a scene, responded by keeping the man isolated and heavily medicated. He too died a painful and lonely death. But he was luckier than a third friend, who was forced to eat food that he wasn't accustomed to, found culturally inappropriate and impossible to swallow. No alternative was provided, and he was left unattended and unmedicated for days.

I'm not easy to horrify, but I was deeply disturbed by the stories I heard. While I listened, I found myself recalling long-forgotten memories of my own grandmother being placed into an aged care facility, begging to be taken out so she could end her life on her own terms. So I agreed on the spot to help Antonio and Jules. I also agreed to act for them in the capacity of the Coffin Confessor.

To make things as easy as possible, and to explain their choice to die with dignity to the world, in addition to my standard contract they provided me with correspondence stating the following:

> We now find ourselves at a road neither of us want to cross. Should we be taken to a home, separated and medicated we know our end will be excruciatingly painful and this is the reason for contacting you. Over the past ten years we have seen first-hand the treatment and demise of close friends who were forced into the aged care system . . . which brings us to why we have chosen to speak with you about our plans to end life as we know it. We are not seeking your assistance with our death nor is this a cry for help – we have a plan in place and will execute this plan at a time we see fit.

The letter finished with official notification that they wanted to engage my services to complete a number of tasks once I had been notified of their deaths. I left, more than happy to take on this responsibility. This was the kind of job only the Coffin Confessor could do, and I would do it pro bono. This one was on me.

* * *

In the days following the meeting with Jules and Antonio, I decided it was time to investigate the aged care system and to see first-hand what they were talking about.

In my past as a PI, I was skilled at getting into institutions and gathering information. A lot of PI work is corporate espionage – the bosses hiring someone to infiltrate the rank-and-file staff of the company, gain their trust, and find out who's got their hand in the till or is otherwise acting against the interests of the company.

I don't know why, but people have a tendency to spill their guts to me. People have always gravitated towards me to talk about whatever is on their minds. It must be that I'm a good listener as I'll sit silently, waiting patiently for hours at a time. I have a resting facial expression that people read as attentive listening. They think I'm hanging on their every word, when in fact I usually have a hundred different things running through my head.

Even if I'm tuned out, I'll be able to recall a conversation word for word later on. It's something that pisses Lara off – I'll tune out while she's talking to me, then when she accuses me of not listening, I'll recite the conversation in its entirety. Verbatim. Which must be a frustrating thing for your spouse to do when you're trying to have a perfectly healthy argument.

So in a short time I befriended a number of nurses and spoke with several cleaning staff at various aged care facilities. They confirmed the allegations made by Antonio and Jules, and together their testimonials painted a grim picture. They all said more or less the same thing: they were understaffed, mismanaged and no one would listen to them, not even the authorities or regulators.

I witnessed residents sitting alone in front of televisions that weren't even switched on. Some were left abandoned in wheelchairs halfway down hallways and forgotten about. To an individual, every single resident I spoke to confided that they were scared of what would happen to them and asked if I could contact their relatives to get them out of there. I was appalled. At the same time, I realised it wasn't the general staff who were to blame. I saw cleaners and carers making meals and giving out food from their own pantries, trying to make life a little better for the residents. Some of the food being served with the resources the home provided was worse than what they used to feed me in Boggo Road.

Then it hit me; these elderly residents weren't in aged care. They were incarcerated. Not even a Royal Commission could expose and fix the numerous issues the aged care system was creaking under. Especially when people are discarding their elderly relatives to a system they have no care or concern about. It's nothing short of abuse, on a systemic, society-wide scale. What we are doing to our elderly today will be their karma tomorrow. The abuse is being hoisted onto the helpless and elderly by a combination of greedy, corrupt corporate aged care companies, and children or next-of-kin who look at their frail parents and see only dollar signs. Older people being abused by parasites and stripped of their human rights is happening all the time. And it's happening everywhere. It's garden-variety economic and domestic abuse, and it's endemic in this country.

I've investigated a number of elder abuse cases over the years and to be honest they're all the same. A son, daughter, or grandchild (sometimes just an opportunistic neighbour) trying to get their filthy fucking hands on money and possessions they think they're entitled to. But thinking isn't knowing and when I'm engaged I make sure everyone involved with these parasites knows *exactly* what they're trying to do.

Investigating elder abuse isn't hard. It's really a matter of seeing where transactions are being made and by whom. It's also best to get as much information about your client as you can, especially their mental capacity. This can make all the difference. If an elderly person has started to decline mentally – and that coincides with them making unusual purchases of clothes, vehicles, jewellery, cash transfers or other gifts – then it's a simple matter of following the paper trail. Visits to hospitals or aged care homes are also easy to check – either through official records, particularly in a post-COVID-19 world, or through speaking to staff.

A few years before I met Antonio and Jules, I was hired to investigate a woman by the name of Amelia who claimed she had grounds for contesting the will of an elderly woman she'd befriended while working in a clothing store some ten years earlier. In her claim, she'd insisted that she'd been the older woman's friend and companion in her final years, until she'd finally passed away after a long battle with dementia. Now Amelia was claiming a six-figure sum that she said the woman had planned to give her in return for her care and friendship.

I was engaged by lawyers acting for the family of the deceased. My instructions were to collect as much evidence as possible in relation to Amelia and the woman she'd allegedly befriended. My investigation revealed that Amelia had been steadily draining the deceased woman's accounts buying incidentals but hadn't visited her so-called friend since she'd been placed into care some three years earlier. Nor had she done a number of other caring acts she claimed to have done in her legal action against the estate. In the end, Amelia was left with nothing but a large bill from her own legal team.

A few weeks after the TEDx talk I was invited to speak at a Royal Flying Doctor Service event where I was told about a man who had bequeathed his home and estate to them. After his death, however, his one-time neighbour contested the dead man's wishes, trying to claim the property. He told the courts he believed he deserved his neighbour's property because he'd given the man lifts to and from a number of appointments and occasionally been grocery shopping for him. What a fucking piece of work that prick was. He'd definitely be a prick I'd loved to have met face-to-face. The only problem is he's not a one-off. There are hundreds just like him, fucking parasites.

No wonder Antonio and Jules wanted to end their lives on their own terms. I understood completely. In some ways, I found them inspirational. It began a process of me really thinking about my own life, and death, and what it would mean to confront that prospect with Lara by my side. I would definitely kill myself before I'm dragged into such a fucking deplorable system that has no care or concern for humanity. Fucked if I'm going to sit in my own filth and not be fed, bathed or cared for. I've always said while I wasn't responsible for my birth I will be for my death. This may sound confronting but it's my death, not yours, and I'll be fucked if I'm going to sit around waiting for a disease to slowly kill me. Or for the treatment to leave me so weak and powerless that I lose the opportunity to really enjoy my last years, months, or weeks.

It's a decision I reached partly through what I learned from Antonio and Jules. A lot of which I owe to their courage. To this day I stay in regular contact with them, hoping they live a little longer, continuing to stare into each other's eyes, but knowing one day I'll get the call. And on that day, I'll be there to help – scattering them in the garden and squashing the bugs and parasites that try to get in the way.

I get why some people decide they don't want to live and would prefer to end their life and join their loved ones in the afterlife. Then there are those like Mitch with the gold necklace, who don't seem to give a shit. The process of moving on is different for everyone. Some do so immediately, some later on in life, while some never do.

Then there are others who find the only way to live again is to become an entirely new person.

* * *

Yvonne was a war widow. Her husband, Terrence, hadn't died in combat, but the army had killed him just the same. He suffered terribly after coming home from two tours. One in Afghanistan and the other on a remote Pacific island that Yvonne had no idea even existed until her husband went there and returned with debilitating PTSD.

Terrence managed it as best he could, buying his dream Indian motorcycle and spending hours on end tinkering with it in his shed. He seemed at peace out there. For a whole day Yvonne might not hear a sound from him, except for the occasional clank or whine of a torque wrench, or when she came in to bring him a cup of tea and two of his favourite biscuits.

One afternoon he'd been unusually quiet when she came out to bring him his afternoon tea. But he wasn't working on his bike. Instead, he was hanging by the neck from the ceiling at the end of a garden hose. Yvonne recalls not moving when she saw him. She didn't drop his biscuits or spill a drop of his tea. She just looked up at him and said, 'Goodbye, my sweet,' went back inside and called for an ambulance.

Police were first on the scene. Yvonne struggled to understand why they were there and not the ambulance, but she was told that with any death the police are always informed and will attend either prior to the ambulance or shortly after.

As an investigator I understand more than most that police have a job to do and while some can seem callous there are many more who have empathy. But truth be told you should never answer questions police ask. You have the right to remain silent and this is your prerogative. Most crimes are solved not because of good police work but because people talk, or they have a co-accused who talks. So the lesson here is *never* have a co-accused and remain silent even if you've done nothing wrong and have nothing to hide. You never know if a cop will have bad intentions and try to pin something on you they suspect you may have done.

Yvonne felt as though she was being interrogated like a murder suspect after her husband's suicide. Before the body was even cold she was questioned about where she was at the time, what she'd been doing, if their finances were okay, or if Terrence was ever violent. This is something she took offence to and decided it best to sit down and say nothing. Her instincts were right.

The police would have been suspicious of Yvonne's outwardly calm demeanour. Which is foolish. Everyone reacts to shock differently and grieves in their own way. But that's where the judgement began, just moments after the death of her husband. It would only spread from there – from the callous police to a misunderstanding family. When it rains, it pours. Yvonne was still in the depths of her grief when she was diagnosed with breast cancer, requiring a double mastectomy.

After her surgery she had a breast reconstruction, giving her the DD cups she had always wanted. She'd never thought about doing it until she was forced to have reconstructive surgery and thought she may as well upgrade while she was at it. Her new breasts gave her the confidence to grow into a new type of person. Or more accurately, many different people, and many different roles.

When Yvonne's husband died it took her a few years to come to terms with it. She knew that she would never fully get over it, and never stop longing for him, but, like most people who become lonely, they eventually turn to dating sites hoping to meet someone like the one they loved and lost. After a few awkward dates, Yvonne realised that whatever happened, she would never find someone to replace her Terrence. There was only one man for Yvonne in the world, and he was dead. But Yvonne didn't need to be Yvonne, not all the time.

A close girlfriend she'd known for decades introduced her to role-playing. The girlfriend described it as a way of keeping safe – in both a physical and emotional sense – and it was the solution to her problems. By meeting men online, specifically to cater for short-term, one-night stands, and in exploring highly particular role-play and fetishes in brief encounters, she was able to step out of the skin of Yvonne the grief-stricken widow, and into new lives – if only for a night.

Yvonne found she loved it. She said she'd never had a bad experience, unlike the bad feelings or experiences she'd had from dating sites. It was companionship of a sort and completely opposite to what she'd loved about her husband. For Yvonne it was a place to meet people, go on dates and explore. In time, she became obsessed with role-playing. She could play the game on her terms. If she walked in and there was anything suss or the man wasn't what she expected, she would just get up and leave without ever meeting them or speaking to them again.

While setting up her dates calendar, Yvonne knew that she could be a different person every night. On Friday night she would not be Yvonne the war widow, but a teacher waiting for her naughty student to punish him. On Saturday night she'd be an air hostess waiting at a bar for her pilot to sweep her off her feet. And on Sunday night she'd play the mistress waiting for her one-night stand to arrive for his weekly blow and go.

Her new breasts, post-surgery, came with a new attitude and new potential for sexual exploration. Yvonne had never thought she'd be able to do what she was doing, and while she was not apologetic she did have regrets. But she was definitely not backwards when coming forwards, so I had to ask why she needed the Coffin Confessor, given that she has as much front as any woman I'd met. This brought us to the shame and judgement of her loved ones.

There's a double standard when it comes to sex in our society it seems: one rule for widower men, another for widows. When gossip got out about Yvonne's new, liberated life, her family and friends became distant. But she continued to live her best life – until about three years after her first cancer diagnosis and major surgery. During a routine physical examination to investigate a lump she'd found, she received the devastating news that the cancer had returned and spread and couldn't be removed or contained. Her doctors gave her less than a year to live.

'I actually thought I'd contracted an STD and had gone to the doctors for some kind of ointment or antibiotic,' she told me with a little chuckle. 'Never trust a pilot who doesn't want to wear a condom. I expected to be told I had the clap, not that I'd be dead within a year.'

Yvonne's sexual liberation that she thought had given her the clap had alienated her from her family. They were socially conservative and couldn't understand why she'd deal with her grief by embracing these new aspects of her personality. Yvonne drifted away from her sister, Kitty, who she loved and missed very much. Their estrangement was in no small part due to Kitty's husband, who was the most judgemental of all. And a hypocrite to boot. When he learned that Yvonne was experimenting with her sexuality, he started lobbying her for sexual favours!

'He tried several times to get a blow job,' Yvonne told me, with some anger. 'And he walked in on me while I was having a shower the night we all went out for his forty-ninth birthday.'

Because of the distance within the family, Yvonne didn't have a chance to tell those she loved how much she loved them. Or those she loved to hate to fuck off. Who better to deliver her eulogy than the Coffin Confessor?

As I sat with Yvonne I noticed a framed picture of a leaf on her bedside dressing table. Under the leaf read '100 Leaves Until We Leave'. I asked what the artwork meant, and she explained that if the average life expectancy is a hundred, then she pictured life as a tree with a hundred leaves on it. Each year, one more leaf will fall. The leaf in the frame was the only one Yvonne had left.

While we talked, I realised that by this system I only had forty-five left. But a hundred is optimistic. None of us know when we're going to go, so we never really know how many leaves are on the tree of our lives until we're in Yvonne's position of having only one remaining year. It's hard to fathom, but that's the way it is. Most of us will only live to around eighty, and some won't even make it that far. For many, we've already lived more life than we ever will again. From the moment we're born, we've already started dying. But how many of us are *really* living like Yvonne?

No one wants to die. But we're all gonna. So ask yourself – how many leaves are left on your tree? What are you going to do? We all live dying. We just go about our lives. And then it's over. So few of us die actually *really* living. And we've got to start doing so, because it's over before you know it. You're never going to see your own funeral – what comes before is the only thing in your control.

While Yvonne didn't want a funeral, she did want a ceremony. After she died, she was cremated and her ashes were scattered in the local creek that she and her late husband would often sit beside and enjoy a picnic of wine and cheese. It was at this place that the mourning family gathered to remember her, and where I read out her eulogy.

My inside woman was a long-time friend of Yvonne's. She'd provided me with constant updates, letting me know when and where Yvonne's ceremony would take place. She was also in charge of scattering the ashes in the creek. Yvonne's instructions were to deliver her eulogy but not speak of her hatred for her sister's husband publicly. Instead, I was to do it privately, and keep that as a face-to-face. Her eulogy was as follows:

> When I was here you were not. And now that you're here I am not. I lived and lost and lived again. I've had ups and downs just like anybody else and I didn't blame anybody else for my choices, especially if they failed me. What I can leave you are these words; live, please live life. Don't put off anything or wait until tomorrow, do it now. I hope there's a heaven, angels, and those I lost waiting to see me. Thank you for loving me, caring about me and being there for me, I'll be watching over you.

Once the eulogy was read and the ashes spread, I approached Kitty, Yvonne's sister, and gave her Yvonne's message. Kitty didn't seem at all surprised by the news. As I walked away she asked me a question. 'Do you know why Yvonne hated my husband so much?'

'I do. And I believe you know too.' It was then that I knew I had the right to tell her. The truth hurt, but it was better off that she knew. There would be anger, but there would also be closure.

With Yvonne now floating down her stream, her friends sharing a wine and cheese platter and her sister contemplating her future, my job was done.

7

Back on the horse

People sometimes ask me to explain the meaning of death. I have to tell them I can't help. The meaning of death, like the meaning of life, is well above my pay grade. But I can tell you what's more important than both of them. It's the same as any gift card in the newsagents. Love. Falling in love with the right person is the single greatest ticket to a good life. It goes the other way too. Falling in love with the wrong person can fuck it all up.

Gail was a married, loving and devoted wife who was loved and liked by all who met her. Ted, her husband, adored her, and his income allowed Gail to work just three days a week as a bookkeeper for a dry-cleaning company. On paper, Gail's life was good, and happy, but she had a secret that was tearing her up.

Gail had read my first book, *The Coffin Confessor*, after a friend told her about me. Something in there seemed to really connect with her. She said she finished it in two days and was compelled to buy the audiobook just so she could hear it read in my voice. I guess she wanted to get a handle on who I was as a person.

When she got in touch, my first impression was of a kind, well-spoken and well-put-together woman. She was in her sixties or early seventies, impeccably dressed, perfectly manicured, with an expensive haircut and a big smile. I got a kind, maternal vibe from her, like you could tell her anything.

But Gail had something to tell *me*, and it wasn't easy for her.

If I'm going to do a job and crash a funeral or intervene on behalf of the dead and dying, I make sure to always have detailed conversations with the client to fully understand what they really need. When clients reach out to me, they often do it in the way you might visit a priest to confess. Only they know I'm not a predator or going to betray them. If they've read my book or heard my story, clients will know that I've seen so many things and heard so many stories, and that they can tell me anything they need to without having to justify it. For some people, all sorts of people, they think I'm the one person in the world they can trust with their secret. That's what it felt like in my first conversation with Gail.

But she had trouble getting her story out. I could tell she carried a lot of baggage from her marriage. Gail and Ted had been together for forty years and like most marriages they'd had their share of ups and downs. Not too long ago, Ted had confessed to an affair he'd had over twenty years earlier with Gail's best friend. Gail had never been able to get over this and it was clear that it had rocked her world in a major way. Recently, her health began to worsen. She lived with a degenerative disease that would eventually leave her incapacitated and in a wheelchair. On top of that, she had a foot condition that caused her chronic pain and she'd been diagnosed with an inoperable malignant tumour. Death wasn't imminent, but it was on the cards, and she wanted me to keep a secret safe until her funeral.

I was intrigued. What Gail was about to confess had me on the edge of my seat but I still wasn't sure what I was being asked to do. She didn't seem like the type who would want revenge and to humiliate her husband, who she clearly loved. Nor did it seem like she was guilty about an affair she'd had that she wanted revealed at the funeral. The more she spoke the more intensely I listened. The service she wanted was for me to quietly, after the funeral, deliver an encrypted video message to her husband. This elegant woman wanted to gently reveal a double life she'd been leading – as a sex worker.

It began soon after she found out about her husband's affair. She'd gone out shopping, then had sat in the car, not wanting to return home, knowing that Ted would be waiting for her and there would be a confrontation. She decided to go to a café and take some time for herself. At the table across from her sat an older lady, who accompanied a young man in a wheelchair. The man was living with significant disability, and while he couldn't talk, he had a badge on his shirt that read: 'Hello, My Name's Barney. Have A Nice Day.'

'Hello, Barney,' Gail smiled at the young man. 'I hope you're having a nice day.'

The woman sitting with Barney thanked her, and introduced herself as Helen. Helen worked as a full-time carer for people with disabilities. Like Gail, she had a naturally caring disposition and the pair hit it off immediately.

After that, Gail headed home for an unhappy conversation with her husband, but she and Helen remained friends. The two women would sometimes catch up at the same café, always with Barney, Helen's disabled client. One Saturday morning, Helen turned up alone, without Barney, and told Gail something that would change her life.

'I get every second Saturday off,' Helen explained.

'That's great, you deserve it. Where's Barney?'

'He's getting his special visitor this morning,' Helen said. 'It's something that he looks forward to all week.'

Gail wasn't sure what Helen meant and asked what a 'special visitor' was. Helen explained this was their cute term for Barney's sex worker. Helen told Gail that people with disabilities still have needs and one of those is intimacy. Since meeting casual partners is difficult when you live with severe disability, many in Barney's position hire a sex worker to come and see them for an hour or so to fulfil the human need for sex, or even just to be touched.

A well-mannered lady like Gail didn't make a habit of looking at strangers and wondering what they got up to in the bedroom. Although she was quite traditional when it came to sex and marital roles, she was surprised to find she wasn't at all put off by the thought of sex work for people with special needs. In fact, she was intrigued. It seemed like an extraordinarily kind thing to do.

For weeks she couldn't stop thinking about it. She googled it several times and grew more and more curious, to the point where she called an agency and volunteered for the job. Just like that, Gail entered the world of disability support work *and* sex work in the same heartbeat.

Back on the horse

Even though she was getting on in years and had more than her fair share of health problems, she'd never really given much thought to what it's like to live with a disability, let alone how a disabled person got their needs met. Even when the body fails, a human being remains a complete human, with all that comes with that. Able-bodied people don't think about it, until they have to. This isn't a criticism. I never gave disability much thought, until the day it came for the one I love most in the world.

* * *

Everyone has bad dreams but mine would haunt your nightmares. I have one dream that won't leave me alone. I'm standing at death's door; literally a physical door to death. It's made of glass but you can't make out what's on the other side, as it's completely dark in there. Pitch black. There's a piece of glass shaped into what looks to be a door handle, and I want nothing more than to take a peek inside, but when I place my hand on the handle it melts like a piece of ice. When I remove my hand the handle reappears, just as it was, but again, when I reach for it, it melts. So instead, I try pushing on the glass but it doesn't budge. Then I knock on it but no one answers. But then, without warning, a lady abruptly pushes past me, opens the door and walks inside. It's so quick I never get a chance to move. I can't go through the door with her, nor do I see what's on the other side. But every time I have this dream I try to manipulate it so as to catch the woman before she enters but I never catch her and it's not long after this that I wake up.

I wonder sometimes if this dream is a message from something beyond my understanding. Perhaps something I'll only understand after my death – if there is in fact anything to be found on the other side of death's door. I do know that there's more to being human that science can currently explain.

I believe we all possess a sixth sense. That said, I don't believe for a second that people can speak to the dead. My personal view is that psychics and mediums profit from those most vulnerable in our society. The gullible and the grieving and a combo of the two. There are those who want to believe more than anything that their loved ones are in a good place and are watching over them. But no living person on this planet knows what's on the other side. Anyone who tells you they do is selling you a fairytale. Probably an expensive one.

I have a real issue with mediums and psychics who pretend to speak to the dead. It's manipulation and nothing short of fraud. I don't speak to the dead. I speak on their behalf. They tell me what they want and I make sure their final wishes are met. In my view, that's about as close to the other side as I'm ever going to get. Until I cross over myself, that is.

We all have experiences in life that make us feel different from other people. Strange occurrences or events that feel supernatural. Some will explore these experiences. Others will ignore them or try to rationalise them. Me, I just continue doing what I do knowing there's something different that separates me from most regular people. I've got this thing. I don't know what to call it, a bit of a superpower maybe, where I can see events before they happen. Bad things. Accidents and tragedies. I can sit in traffic and someone will pass me by and for no apparent reason I can see their death. It's like I've made up some bullshit story in my head about that particular person. A person I've never met nor may ever meet, but for some twisted reason they become a slow-motion short film flashing before my eyes. As fast as it came, it's gone. It's something I've had ever since I was little. I'd see a neighbour climb into their car and know that they were going to have an accident later that day. Even in a crowd I could spot someone who had something terrible coming their way. Not the details, but just that they were due some bad luck.

It's very weird, and I can't explain it, but it's served me well. Especially when I was in jail. I'd be in the exercise yard and I'd see another prisoner come in and feel in my gut that something terrible was going to happen. So I'd leave and go somewhere safe and, sure enough, not long afterwards, the knives would come out and the place would be a bloodbath.

Later in life, I'd try to warn people when I could tell something bad was going to happen, but it was impossible. People just thought I was crazy. Back when I was working with a construction crew building roads, just after I got out of jail, there was this one guy I really liked, but every time I spoke to him I would get this flash, just for a few seconds, of him lying crushed under an excavator. I told him, 'Hey, listen, be careful around that excavator next time you're on shift,' but there was no way to say that I'd had a vision without sounding like a madman. So I could never find a way to warn him and sure enough, one day at work the excavator rolled over, cresting a hill and right onto the poor guy.

While I was in Cairns I recall telling a lady to drive safely after she bumped into me walking to her car in the car park. I had a flash of her being involved in an accident and felt compelled to warn her. She gave me a funny look, continued to her car, and then climbed into the passenger seat. Her male companion got behind the wheel, reversed out, and rammed straight into a motorbike, badly injuring the rider, while the man and the woman in the car were safe.

Even when I see something bad in the future that will affect a friend or a family member, it's never easy to warn them. Especially if I can't see exactly what it is, but just have a premonition that something bad is going to happen. I can't even warn myself properly.

The other day I was driving along the highway and I saw this bloke in the rear-view mirror absolutely flying up the road. He was swerving all over the shop. *He's going to hit someone*, I thought. Sure as shit. It wasn't just that he was driving like a maniac, I knew in my bones that he was going to cause an accident. I tried to get away from him and switched over into the far lane. We came to a set of lights and I slowed down, relieved I'd avoided this guy, then right at the last possible second, he swerved into my lane, going full speed and hit me up the arse.

I couldn't believe it. My car is tough, an old muscle car, but it took a good whack. The other driver was a mess. It turned out he was on drugs, with no insurance and driving an unregistered vehicle. I was pissed off, but I saw it as lucky. Because if he hadn't hit me, he might have ploughed straight into a little plastic hatchback in front of me with two women and a back seat full of young children instead.

So I felt like I was warned about the accident, but I still couldn't avoid it. If it's a superpower, it's a pretty fucking ordinary one in terms of practicality!

My wife, Lara, has known about this our whole life together, because we've been together since she was fifteen. And sometimes it scares her. She'll often say if I have a premonition but I can't warn someone, that I should, 'Just plant the seed, then.'

'Okay, dear, what do you mean by that?'

'If you know something is going to happen to someone, just tell them to be careful out there.'

I obviously can't go up to people, even people I know well, and say, 'Listen, I've had a vision that you're going to crash your Honda Civic the next time it rains.' But I try to give good advice. 'It's raining out there for the first time in a while, the roads will be slippery, so take care on the corners, yeah?'

It's not that easy. Sometimes you can't avoid disaster, even if you're sure it's coming. Even when it's coming for your loved ones.

* * *

Lara and I have horses. Since we were teenagers, raising our kids had been our sole and most important focus in life. From the minute Lara picked me up from prison at the end of my sentence and the start of our life together, we'd called each other 'Mum' and 'Dad'. To our kids, of course, but also to each other. It's funny how names can define us. These days, we call each other 'LaLa' and 'Popeye' due to our six grandchildren.

We spent pretty much every minute building a home for our kids, but now that they were off starting their own lives, we experienced a very strange moment. It felt weird to call each other 'Lara' and 'Bill'. Our first night alone in the house, I remember looking at her across the dinner table and saying, 'Hey, Lara.'

'You haven't called me that since we were teenagers.'

'I know, right? This feels really weird.'

There was a pause, and then Lara suddenly said, 'Look, we've got to find something to do with our lives, otherwise we're going to implode. And it's not going to be good.' I knew she was right. So we started discussing what would do with our downtime, now that we had downtime for the first time in our lives.

Lara loved horses, but we'd never been able to afford them. When the kids left home, and there was a little bit of spare money, suddenly a horse was a possibility. We found a beautiful horse named Bert, a name I despised as it was my grandfather's, so we decided to call him Buddy. Buddy was our first horse, and Lara entered the world of horse riding. Soon she started trail riding and discovered a whole community of riders. She was really talented, a natural rider.

I never had the knack so instead I went to the gym and thought about what I really liked. It took me a while to work it out. For a few years I got into motorbikes and tinkered with them on and off. I enjoyed it and it kept me busy. But I never had that really committed passion for riding motorbikes that Lara had with her horses. God, she loved her horses. I did too, but not to ride, just to hang out with. It was a highlight when we'd visit the property where the horse lived with seven others. I'd go to feed them and they'd all come up to me and say hello. It was very therapeutic. I've always loved animals. To be honest, I like animals more than people most days. But there's something extra special about a horse – they are so intelligent and majestic and just . . . cool. They remind me of dinosaurs; big and placid, but also strong. In a moment they could take off and tear you apart.

When we could finally afford a property of our own we decided that Buddy needed a friend, as horses are very social creatures.

We found one that was being kept in a shitty little field, and it was just miserable. This poor animal was being neglected. But Lara, who has a great instinct, said, 'She's not a good horse. Her physique and temperament are no good for trail riding. The vet bills could be out of control.'

'Yeah,' I said, 'but look at her face.' The poor thing looked so hopeful that we'd take her away and look after her that we just had to.

We ended up buying a third horse because Lara wanted to explore and experience a rodeo event called barrel racing. So she bought three-year-old stallion named Zipper. He was a world horse. We had him gelded but that didn't take the edge off. He was a feisty thing, beautiful to look at, and very competent. Lara loved him, and as he was young she thought she could tame him and turn him into something great. But I knew he was dangerous from the moment I met him. Just how dangerous, I was about to find out. Or to be more accurate, Lara was.

Over the years we always bought the best horse-riding gear you can get on the market. We've got our own horse float, saddles, bridles, whatever a rider could want. But now and again Lara would borrow someone else's gear. She'd be at a friend's place, or it was more convenient to borrow a float than drive all the way back to our property to pick up ours. I couldn't say why, but every time she did this, it upset me. It just felt wrong.

While on a three-day trail ride through the bush in South East Queensland, she borrowed another rider's saddle and put it on Zipper. As I say, this was a good horse, but he could still be a bit unruly at times. I got the familiar sense of dread. It's terrible, because on one level I knew something bad was going to happen, but on another level I couldn't change how it was going to play out.

I was told that Lara was riding the horse on the borrowed saddle, when out of nowhere Zipper reared up and threw her off. That was bad enough. But then the half-tonne horse fell and landed on top of Lara, crushing everything below the waist. She was in the middle of nowhere and they had to get a CareFlight rescue helicopter to airlift her to Brisbane. Not only that, it was right in the middle of COVID-19, so the hospital was under strict quarantine. Security would not let me in, and I had no contacts at that particular security company.

At first I thought about impersonating a doctor, but then it occurred to me that I could just *pretend* to be security. It helps that I've got more front than Myer. Security not only allowed me access but escorted me through the hospital to Lara's ward. I could see her from behind a large glass window. I caught the attention of a nurse, who was able to give Lara a bag of clothes and, more importantly, a mobile phone. It was traumatic seeing her lying there but I knew she was in good care.

Her injuries were terrible. A broken hip, minor fractures and serious nerve damage, which has left her with a permanent disability known as drop foot. She underwent surgery and had pins and plates and screws inserted into her legs to save them. She was in hospital for five months – in a wheelchair, then on crutches, then a cane – and slowly she learned how to walk again. But the doctors said she'd have a permanent disability on her left side.

When she eventually came home from hospital, she was taking too much medication and started experiencing bad chest pains and then all of a sudden she passed out. I called 000 and told the operator, 'I think my wife's having a heart attack and it's not good!' I described the symptoms, and the operator sent for an ambulance. All the while, she kept me on the line. 'Okay, it sounds like she's having a heart attack. Keep monitoring her. If she does go into cardiac arrest, you're gonna have to do CPR.'

'No problem. I can do that.' Luckily the ambulance wasn't too far away. Although we're fairly isolated on the farm, the townships are only six minutes away.

For Lara to come home and then turn around and have to go back into hospital was a totally fucked-up situation. It was twice as hard the second time. I thought I'd lost her twice in the space of a year. It was brutal. The worst time of my life. Worse than prison, worse than my childhood. Because it wasn't my wellbeing on the line. The stakes were much, much higher.

But now she's back and she's great – walking and even horse riding again. Quite literally, she's back on the horse. It was a tough period, but at the same time, I don't know anyone who could have handled it better. If it wasn't for the way Lara is – her temperament and resilience – it would have been a lot worse. She doesn't let things get to her. I think I've rubbed off on her a lot in that way. She's done the same for me. They say behind every great man is a great woman. Well, I'm married to the greatest woman on the planet. She isn't going to let a little thing like being crushed by a massive horse stop her from doing what she loves. Kudos to her for that.

We rehomed the wild horse that injured her, but otherwise there's no ongoing drama. It wasn't the horse's fault. Accidents happen. If a skydiver jumps out of a plane and something goes wrong, you don't blame the plane. You can't stop accidents from happening. Your only choice is how you respond to them.

Lara has always been an inspiration to me, and never more so than the past couple of years. A giant horse falling on her could crush every bone in her legs, sure. But it couldn't crush her spirit.

* * *

My client Gail had become a specialist sex worker, helping the disabled, partly because of what it did for her own mental health and self-esteem. She told me this, all in a rush over coffee, at our first meeting.

I'm rarely surprised, but I wasn't expecting this. At first glance, Gail did not strike me as a sex worker. But I didn't judge. I respect the hard work behind it. And I've spent enough time in rehab wards and disability support facilities to understand how important her job was.

As the saying goes, prostitution is the oldest profession on the planet. But it's seen by many as a dirty, disgusting and degrading way of making money. But that's ignorance talking. People do it for all sorts of reasons. I've met the whole gamut over the years. As a private investigator, I spent years following deadshit husbands who were stepping out on their wives with prostitutes. I've known prostitutes turned private investigators, who use their skills from the first job to get the second job done. As the Coffin Confessor, I've met my share of people who want to confess to hiring sex workers, as well as the other side – people who survived through sex work because it was a last resort, or it was just the best path

Back on the horse

for them. But I'd never met anyone who did it for the reasons Gail did.

She spoke about the pleasure she took in meeting clients at their homes and pleasuring them. After her first job, where she spent intimate time with a paraplegic for whom this was the highlight of their week, she was struck by how much she enjoyed the work. She was a kind woman and felt she was performing a service to those in need that is never spoken about because it's taboo. On the other hand, she enjoyed it herself to an extent she didn't expect.

Gail was a woman with her own needs. She and her husband had always had a great relationship – or so Gail thought – but they were quite traditional in their gender roles, right down to sex. I got the impression it was a very meat-and-three-veg sort of relationship – a lot of missionary – and something as simple as a bit of cowgirl was threatening to Gail's husband.

Gail always wanted something more and she had always wanted to experiment with being more dominant in the bedroom. But she was too embarrassed to tell her husband this. She'd tried instigating certain things that she hoped Ted would warm to, but he didn't, and her self-esteem waned. It got even worse after his affair. It turned out that giving pleasure to those who needed it more than anyone was the perfect way of her getting the pleasure she always wanted.

As Gail explained all this to me, it made perfect sense. I'd never given this line of work a moment's thought, but I was 100 per cent on her side.

It's natural for humans to want sex and to explore their sexuality. Just because they happen to be trapped in a body that doesn't function in the same way as the average person does, doesn't mean they should be ostracised or left never knowing the enjoyment of sex. If both sides are getting something out of it, and it's easy to achieve, then why would you resign yourself to celibacy if you had a choice? Let's leave that to the fucking priests. Although I'm pretty sure we all know where most of them go to fulfil their needs.

Gail found fulfilment on multiple levels with her side hustle, and I thought, *Good on ya*. She was good at it, and built a loyal clientele, and made decent money. After a while, she rented a small apartment that she would use to meet clients. She used her earnings to fit it out with high-end quality furniture, with a sort of beach-house nautical theme, which she'd always wanted. Carers would drop off their clients, then come back and pick them up much happier after a couple of hours in Gail's company.

To explain her long absences, she told her husband that she'd been offered a part-time bookkeeping position at a factory and that she had to work from both home and the office, but it would mean extra money coming in.

Over time, Gail also invested in a professional wardrobe – lingerie, costumes, wigs, toys – which I think she got more pleasure out of than her clients. Wearing these props allowed her to pretend to be someone else, to put on another personality, perhaps of the woman she would have been if she'd been able to live a freer life. It gave her the power to become a special kind of hero for the disadvantaged, disabled and those with special needs.

Living a secret life isn't uncommon and there are a few people I've met who'd jump at the opportunity, if the risks weren't so high.

Gail had taken that chance, and in doing so was finding a way to recover from the hurt and shame of her husband's infidelity. She'd been devastated by his affair and would have left decades earlier when she'd found out about it, but couldn't because Ted had all the money and all the power.

This was back when most women stayed at home and most men went to work. Gail never had any money or anything for herself. At the time of her husband's affair, she didn't even have her own bank account. That's how she grew up, and that's how her adult life was. She was trapped by the realities of patriarchy and money. Worse, she was alone. She'd lost her best friend when Ted started fucking around, and she'd never really had one since. That, along with a man who really didn't show any interest in her no matter how much she tried to get his attention, chipped away at her self-esteem. Gail knew Ted was getting it from elsewhere but eventually she stopped caring. She knew she'd done all she could to make the marriage happy and that a divorce would mean losing her home, maybe her pets, and definitely her finances, which were mainly Ted's. So she'd stayed, and they'd moved on, in a way, but it still ate her up inside. Decades of anger and frustration built up until she finally did something about it.

'I didn't want to become invisible like so many women I know do after they turn fifty,' she told me.

There were certain things that empowered her and one of them was having her own money. The other was the freedom to not worry about what she was doing because her husband had hurt her so badly in the past. Putting on a costume and feeling powerful and desired was a way for her to take back the power of her own sexuality.

You'd think that providing all those happy endings would mean, well, a happy ending, but Gail was torn up by guilt. Not so much by what she was doing, but that she couldn't share it with her life partner. She'd never told her husband and couldn't bring herself to. So while the job made her happy, she was also terrified that he would find out and be hurt. There were plenty of people out there who knew what she was up to. The agency who got her into it, her clients, all their care workers. Even in big cities, people talk, and it scared her. She worried what it would do to her husband to find out his wife was sleeping with other men, and didn't want him to feel like that. The trust was broken in the marriage, and this, in its own way, was her way of repairing it. But it wasn't a perfect solution.

As the conversation went on, I could tell Gail had been through some serious mental health challenges. She confessed that at times she'd considered taking her own life. She'd sought out counselling and psychologists but none of them was of any help.

While I'm no shrink, I have counselled a number of people in financially and emotionally abusive situations. I've come to believe that if a person is set on taking their own life then there is nothing you can say or do to stop them. Much as I wish I could.

* * *

I once had a client who wanted me to be her living suicide note. She had decided she wanted to die and wanted her family to understand the reasons why. Instead of leaving a note she asked me to go and tell her family so I could answer their questions. It would have to be the world's first suicide with a scheduled Q&A after. Safe to say, I was reluctant.

'That's not something I can do,' I said. Instead, I recommended a good counsellor I knew. 'I probably can't convince you otherwise, but things *will* get better. This seems like a personal crisis.'

'No, I think this is something you *can* do,' She insisted. 'I want this to be personal.'

In the end, we reached a compromise. She agreed to get help, and I agreed to take a letter she'd written, to be read out to the family at her funeral if she decided to go through with it. Ultimately, I thought, *Well, you know what, I am the Coffin Confessor. And I am confessing people's secrets beyond the grave, so who am I to refuse this request?* Legally, if someone wants to kill themselves, I can't stop them. It's not like I can drag them kicking and screaming to a psychiatric ward. I can't help them, although believe me, I've tried in the past.

Up to the age of around seventeen I came close to taking my own life several times. Once when I was standing on a ledge of a high-rise building; once when I attempted to slash my wrists; once when I put a plastic bag over my head and jumped into a pool. There may have been other attempts but I don't recall them now. Every now and again a memory I've repressed will pop up and I'll think, *Oh, fuck, that's horrible. I buried you for a reason!*

So I know what I'm talking about here. I also know that had I succeeded I would have missed out on experiencing true love and a life worth living. Fortunately, I never managed to end my own life, and now can continue in the knowledge that we all have only one life and I'm going to live it, not pack up my ball early and go home.

I've learned that the best I can do for people who tell me they want to die is urge them to go and get some help, because

I know, first-hand, that those suicidal impulses will pass. If you have the potential to wake up happy tomorrow, a week from now, a decade later, and that never happens because you went and offed yourself? You'd feel pretty fucking silly, and your loved ones are going to be pretty fucking devastated.

This particular client ended up taking her life not long after my first book came out. I gathered the family together and read out the suicide note that she'd asked me to deliver. It was a pretty dismal turnout. Only a few people, and they seemed to resent even being there. My guess is my client hoped this moment would give her family some closure. That they'd cry a bit and then say something like, 'This is terrible, at least now we know why she took her own life. We can move on. Thank you so much.'

Yeah, that would have been a great story, but it's not how it panned out, unfortunately.

The brother was the first to speak. 'She should have done it years ago.'

He was a real fucking piece of work. The dad wasn't much better. His wife, my client's mother, had died a few months earlier and I believe that this was a big part of why my client took her own life. It messed her up. It had certainly messed up the dad who seemed more depressed about his wife's death. The death of his daughter was an afterthought. There was no real reaction to the note, no real remorse for the opinions and hurt expressed in the letter about how they'd treated her. In my professional opinion, they didn't give a fuck. My client deserved better. A fucked-up and sad scenario, but they exist and there's no point sugar-coating it.

Then again, I guess it's all subjective. Some people really value life and others don't. I've always said the family I've created is far better than the family I came from. My current family is everything to me, and in my eyes they are the most important people on the planet. At the same time, I hate the family I was born into – a nest of degenerates and abusers. To be fair, they hate me too. If I were to die and someone went and told my birth family they would probably give the same answer: 'About fucking time. He should have gone years ago.'

* * *

So I knew where Gail was coming from, and instead of preaching and giving my two cents, I just sat and listened to her pour out her heart. When she was done, I promised I would help her deliver a message to her husband, Ted, after her death. She gave me a business card that had a password and login details to her own pre-recorded encrypted video message. What was on the video was between her and her husband, but I took it to be a full confession about her job, and her reasons for doing it.

I'd never met anyone who did sex work for the pleasure it gave them, but why not? I live and let live, I don't pass judgement, except on those who judge others without walking a mile in their shoes. Fuck them. I'm with the Gails of the world, living her life and ending it the way she was going to end it, on her own terms.

I very rarely think about my clients after we're done. The way the job works, once we've signed a contract, if all goes well, I'll only see them again once they're dead. But Gail is an exception.

I find myself thinking of her and being grateful that she's in the world and doing the work that nobody else is kind enough to do. Every so often, I'll send her a quick text asking if she's okay. To this day, she still replies with the same message: 'AOK'.

8

The confessional

As the Coffin Confessor, I've been privileged to witness some beautiful stories of love and marriage. I've seen the ideal scenario of a happy marriage, where the two partners lend the best parts of themselves and use that potential to grow over the years into the greatest possible people, both together and as individuals. These are the best love stories, even if they end in tragedy. All love stories will end tragically, after all, because at least one of the major characters is going to fucking die. It's what comes before the inevitable that is important.

A good love story usually means a good life, one that the Coffin Confessor is called in to celebrate the end of after a good innings. On the other hand, I've seen some real fucking horror shows. Some people come to me with confessions that are so out of order they wouldn't dare confess them to a friend, or a psychologist, or even their priest. So they come to me. People like Sarah.

* * *

'I wish my husband was dead,' Sarah told me from her deathbed. 'I've wanted him dead for so, so long.' Her tone wasn't angry, or bitter, or full of malice. Just a little sad and disappointed, maybe. Sarah wanted her husband to die. Fact of the matter. That's all. Not because he was a mean bastard. Not drunk or abusive or manipulative or rotten in one of the thousands of ways shitty husbands can be. No, Jacob was a perfectly fine husband. He worked full-time in a career that provided for a white-picket-fence dream home a short walk from Sydney's Bronte Beach.

Their only child, a daughter, went to a prestigious local high school and was looking forward to going to boarding school for her senior years. She was smart, popular and as hardworking as her father. From the outside, Sarah had the perfect life. But she couldn't stand it, but nor could she imagine separating from her husband. She reached a point where it seemed like the only solution was for *him* to die. *What a piece of work*, I thought at our first meeting. *Surely I'm talking to a psychopath here.*

Sarah was a chameleon. When I first met her she presented as a beautiful, well-dressed and educated, classy woman. A loving wife and mother. She could fit into any class of society without an issue. If you dropped her into a new social group, she adapted instantly. She even spoke differently depending on where she was and who she was with. And it seemed she wanted to be with everyone, minus their clothes. I'm no psychiatrist, but as she gave me her deathbed confession, I suspect 'Sarah the chameleon' was also 'Sarah the nymphomaniac'.

Sarah wanted Jacob gone so she'd be free to live out her sexual fantasies – which were extensive, and highly detailed. Her fantasies were so graphic, insatiable and specific that she knew

The confessional

it would break her husband's heart if she were ever to confess how she felt. So she repressed her secret desires to the point where she thought she would be happier with her husband dead rather than disappoint him with the truth.

But irony is a bitch, and Sarah found out that she would be dying long before Jacob. She'd been an enthusiastic sun-tanner her whole life, but now it had come back to bite her. An unchecked mole had become a melanoma, which had metastasised, and the cancer was walking her to death's door very, very fast.

Sarah had heard about the Coffin Confessor on Facebook, and she was intrigued about what might be done and said after someone's death. She didn't give it any real thought, though – until she was given a terminal diagnosis. Which is how I came to be sitting with her, listening to her confession.

She said she'd get off by flirting and having men admire her beauty, but insisted she had never fucked around behind Jacob's back. However, she did feel a little guilty about flirting outrageously with men and then going home to make love to Jacob, all the while thinking of the blokes who'd shown interest in her.

'Tell me your opinion,' she asked me in a flirtatious tone. 'Do you think I'm *naughty* for doing that?'

'I don't have an opinion,' I said flatly.

'None at all? You don't think that's *bad*?'

'Sarah, I couldn't care less. If you go out to work up your appetite and then go home to eat? That's your business, not mine.'

Sarah pouted. Even on her deathbed she was flirting. I could feel the energy in the room. She was trying to create a frisson – confessing how she loved nothing more than going to the beach and lying topless, rubbing sunscreen over her body, while pretending not to notice the men staring at her. Other times she'd go out – to a party, to the shops – wearing a little dress without panties and prance around hoping the wind would blow it up over her thighs.

'I like to know I can give a man an erection without touching him,' she purred, looking me squarely in the eye.

'Ma'am,' I said, 'they're men. A bumpy bus ride will give some guys an erection.' I added that any man she could seduce with a look would be thinking with his dick and the biggest mistake a man can make is to let his dick think for him. 'There's not enough blood in the male body to run the heart, brain and an erection at the same time, so to follow your dick's orders is a sure way to ruin a relationship, lose your wealth and fuck up your life.'

'Oh yes?' Sarah wouldn't give up. 'Do you have first-hand experience with this?'

'I was a private investigator for many years. I've seen enough men blow up their lives over a five-minute blow job in a back alley to last a lifetime.'

It's true. I just can't understand why a man would allow his dick to control his actions, but I've seen it time and time again. I was once hired to follow the husband of a prominent, well-known lady. Not only was she prominent and well-known, but she was gorgeous – she had beauty, brains and money, and she was devoted to her husband and family. Unfortunately, her husband was devoted to his next fuck, which nine times out of ten wasn't her. After many years and even more suspicions she knew it, and hired me to find proof. It took many years of her growing suspicious, but only a few days for me to bring back proof of her husband's infidelity.

Sarah had almost the opposite problem. She thought about fucking around all the time, but never acted on it directly. Nevertheless, it had ruined her life. She confessed to starting arguments with Jacob for no reason other than she just wanted her space. She knew that either she or Jacob would storm out of the house, and she would be left alone for a day or two, giving her space and time to enjoy her secret inner world of exhibitionism.

I couldn't count the number of times I've heard arguments being started for no real reason. I've listened to women say they've instigated an argument to avoid having sex with their partner. Which seems like a fair enough reason to pick a fight. Honesty is probably a better policy, but I'm not the horny police. Men also start arguments for no reason. Fuck, just writing that made me laugh. Truth be told there's always a reason a man will start an argument and it's usually because of something he feels guilty about. Maybe his partner is rejecting his sexual advances because he's not taking care of his physicality. Maybe he's hiding his finances – spending money on other relationships or gambling issues.

It's not that women can't or don't have these issues. It's just that in my experience most women will talk about their problems, confess to a friend, and try to work on that behaviour. Men will start an argument to avoid having a difficult conversation, 100 per cent. But you can be sure as shit a man won't start an argument because he doesn't want sex.

Now Sarah didn't need excuses to avoid sex with Jacob. Death was imminent and she planned to die without ever sharing her secret desires with her husband. But at the same time she wanted him to know about them, but only after she was gone.

Perhaps it would help him to move on without her – to know that their entire marriage she had fantasised about fucking other men . . .

She engaged me to deliver this message after her funeral – that she had truly loved her husband, but at the same time could never reconcile her love for him with her insatiable desires for other men, and so had fantasised not just about sex with strangers, but about burying him so she was free to go buck wild.

What a request. I considered how it would feel for poor Jacob, to have this news delivered in person by a stranger, especially by some big, strange bloke with an inscrutable expression.

From a very young age I was told I had a look that was near impossible to read. It was a locked expression of hurt, anger and aggression. Today people call it 'resting bitch face' but personally I don't see it. But I could see it wasn't the best face to deliver this unhappy news to Jacob. While I often say I have no care or concern for those left behind, the truth is I do. I just can't show it very easily.

In the past, whenever I was hurt or happy, my look never really changed. I can only put this down to me not wanting to show any emotions to my abusers as it would only give them more power over me in their sick fucking minds. It's a survival mechanism. When I was in a street fight or boxing I never showed my pain despite how much it hurt, because nothing intimidates your opponent more than when they break your nose and you don't so much as blink. What I do know is the look I have has got me out of more situations than it has got me into – especially when I was in jail. The look I gave had people who were thinking about sticking a knife in me second-guess whether that was a good idea.

The confessional

I've never been one to show emotion and I believe if I did, I'd probably be lying in the foetal position, crying at all the shit I've gone through, heard and seen. I never even show positive emotions. When I was excited to see Lara or someone I was close to, I never showed much emotion. At times it makes me wonder why they gravitated towards me in the first place. Lara often tells me to smile – 'it takes fewer muscles to smile than it does to frown' – and I'll frown because I wasn't even aware I was frowning.

With that in mind, I encouraged Sarah to write it all down in her own words. That way Jacob could read it in private and I wouldn't be the one telling him his wife was as mad as a fucking cut snake. As a husband I'd find it hard to digest, especially when the news of your wife's secret double fantasy life was delivered by a complete fucking stranger.

Sarah died not long after from the cancer that ravaged her body. I attended the funeral and, after a respectful wait, I gave Jacob the letter she'd left for him. He didn't open it in front of me, nor did he ask any questions. He just took the letter, thanked me and walked away.

* * *

This was early on in my role as the Coffin Confessor and back then I thought surely Sarah was a one-in-a-million head case; to feel trapped in a marriage and never confess her real desires, much less act on them. But I would soon discover that she was far from alone. In fact, I discovered hundreds of people live day in day out wishing their partner were dead. Not only because they're in an abusive relationship, or they'd done something unforgivable, but because they wanted to be single and couldn't stand the thought of their loved one being with someone else. Sounds pretty fucked up but truth be told it's a thought that goes through the minds of many people who are trapped in toxic relationships. They truly love their partner but would rather see them dead than break their heart by being with someone else.

I knew a guy in Cairns who lost his wife suddenly and not two days later came into the nightclub I was managing and hooked up with a gorgeous-looking bartender. The following night he stopped by and hooked up with one of the male security guards. It was as if his wife had never existed. But when you spoke to him he was full of grief. To me he was full of crap. I understand that everyone deals with grief in their own way, and there's no 'wrong' way to go about it, but I'm pretty certain that fucking your way through the queue lining up at both genders of toilets ain't the 'right' way to honour the dead. I often think of that guy when I think about Cairns. Although, there was another job up north and if there ever could be a model for the 'right' way to grieve, that would have to be it.

* * *

We've all been to funerals or gravesites with flowers in hand. But what if it was reversed and the deceased gave you flowers, cards or gifts from beyond the grave?

I once received an email from a woman named Louise who also lived in Cairns. I knew the place well, given I'd worked there as a bouncer, bodyguard and manager back in the 1990s. Cairns is the gateway to one of the seven wonders of the world, the

Great Barrier Reef, so a mecca for backpackers. And where backpackers go, booze follows, and where booze flows freely in the tropical heat and high humidity, tempers rise, and fights ensue. I remember it as being a hard place, with hard weather and harder men. So Louise's tender request was not one I expected.

Over a Zoom call, Louise told me she didn't want revenge, or a score settled, or for me to confess a dark secret at her funeral. She simply wanted me to visit her widowed husband, Shane, on his birthday and deliver a bottle of his favourite wine, along with a card she'd written on her deathbed, a final message of love from beyond the grave. It wasn't something I'd been engaged to do before, but I thought it a very nice and romantic gesture from a loving and devoted wife. Naturally, I said yes, and on the allotted day, I jumped on a flight to the tropics.

I arrived in Cairns and as predicted the heat and humidity hit me like a wet, hot towel. From the moment I arrived I wanted to leave but I had to admit, apart from the heat, the town was very different to what I remembered. It was family friendly with water parks, cafés and bistros lining the esplanade. Nearly every person I walked past had a smile on their face. A vast difference from the violent shithole and bloodbath I lived in during the 1990s.

As I headed towards Redlynch, the northern suburb where Shane lived, I noticed familiar places, but there were many more new builds that I'd never seen. It had me intrigued just how much somewhere can change when you haven't been there for twenty or more years.

Pulling up to Louise and Shane's house, I grabbed the bottle of red and the envelope containing Louise's card and walked up to the entrance. Behind a security door, the main door was wide open. Ceiling fans were spinning like helicopter blades in a vain effort to do something about the humidity. I knocked loudly and called out, 'Hello! I'm looking for Shane.'

'In here!' came the reply. 'Come on in.'

Shane must have thought I was a visiting friend or relative, so I stood on the threshold and waited for him to appear and unlock the security door. As it swung open, I told him who I was and what I was doing on his doorstep. Shane invited me in and offered me a cold glass of water and a Great Northern beer, both of which I accepted. I don't particularly like beer, but I didn't want to be rude, and besides, I'd never been thirstier. We sat, drinking in the dining room while I explained how Louise had engaged my services prior to her death, and asked me to deliver these gifts. I placed the red wine and envelope on the table in front of him.

He picked up the card, read it, and his eyes filled with tears. He then started to laugh as tears cascaded down his cheeks. 'I should probably have seen this coming,' he giggled after a while. 'Me and Lou saw you on the telly, talked about you, and even listened to some interviews you've done on podcasts. I should have known Lou was planning something like this. Thank you.'

'It's my pleasure. Your wife seemed like a good woman. This was all her idea.'

With that, I thanked Shane for his time and the beverages and got up to leave. When I was finally back home, and out of the crazy humidity, I shared the story of Louise delivering a gift from the grave. After that I received a deluge of emails and requests asking for similar services. And so the Coffin Confessor Afterlife Gifts and Delivery Services was born. It turns out that a service helping people confess their undying love, even after death, was something the world was crying out for. So in that way, through the work of the Coffin Confessor, Louise lives on, brightening the lives of those who have lost their loved ones.

* * *

I hadn't met Louise face to face other than via a Zoom call. She spoke about her battle with cancer, something I'd witnessed many times before, but it never gets easier seeing it up close. I can't imagine the pain and suffering cancer patients go through, let alone those who know the treatment is futile. There must be nothing more crushing than being told the radiotherapy and chemotherapy that has ruined your body isn't killing the fucking disease, and the inevitable is just a few weeks away.

I've lost people I really liked and cared for to cancer. I'm not alone given most people have been touched by it in some way or another. I'm not scared of much in this world, but I can't stand the thought of what would happen if I were to ever develop cancer. I've often thought about how I might die. Not when or where but how. Will my death be violent? Perhaps I'll be murdered on the job. Killed in a car accident. Or will I die doing what I love – spending time at home, holding hands with the love of my life. I know this much: I won't die from a terminal disease. I won't allow it. I'll be gone long before I become a burden. There's no way I'll be lying in a fucking hospice bed awaiting death to visit me; I'll be running right through death's fucking door announcing my arrival.

Those I lost from cancer all went through treatment and I've decided if I get it there'll be no treatment for me. I want to live my last weeks, months or years without the constant pain and mobility issues. I want to eat, drink, travel and make love to my wife until I'm in my death throes. And if those things force me to my deathbed earlier than expected at least I'll be able to say I had fun on the way out. Because if there's one takeaway I've got from witnessing countless deaths as the Coffin Confessor, it's this: death is inevitable. It's coming for you right now. So have fun while you're still alive. And, if possible, help your loved ones have fun after you're gone.

* * *

Different people, cultures, faiths all see death differently. Some see it as a passage to another life. Others see it as a new beginning. Me, I see it as the end of life and nothing more. Possibly there is another world, an afterlife beyond, but I believe in this one. I believe that in the act of dying, it's the final moments and last wishes of the individual that are of most importance. This allows me to feel empathy for those who are on their deathbed, which empowers me to help them die in the manner they want – whatever their culture or religion. Death is the universal that connects all cultures. But how people connect to death varies wildly.

I've crashed a Māori funeral, an Irish funeral and a Fijian funeral, and while they're all different cultures with different values, they all embraced the fact that the role I was playing was not of my choosing but one their loved one had wanted. Respect must be shown to the deceased no matter how controversial it may be. I understand people from other cultures and religions objecting to my service, but it's not their funeral. I'm there for the guy or gal in the box. In cultures other than the one I grew up in, people seem to respect the wishes of the dead.

Crashing the Fijian funeral, I had a rare moment of doubt. When I rocked up, there were all these big guys in grass skirts carrying banana leaves. I was faced with the fact that I was stepping into this whole other culture. They had their own rituals, their own way of doing things, a different idea of family. I'm very happy to get up and cause a scene at a funeral in a church – I know the ropes and I know better than anyone the odds that any given church has let a child abuser get away with it – but I didn't have that background here, so didn't know what was in store.

I thought that it might be confronting for them, to have this random white guy stand up and do his thing. And at first, yeah, there was some hostility, and I realised that if a fight were to break out it would be me versus a combined two tonne of Fijian mourners, but the second they heard that I was hired by the deceased, the vibe totally changed. Once they knew I wasn't some prick that an outsider had hired, they got it instantly. They respected the wishes of the deceased, and just went with it. They even gave me a crash course on their burial rites.

'This is what we eat before the funeral, these are the specific foods we eat, and how we prepare them. After the burial we have wine, and at this specific time we'll have apple cider.' They brought me along for the whole ride. It was fascinating, exploring another culture that, frankly, seemed to have a much healthier attitude to death than the shit I grew up with. Even though I'm an atheist, I grew up in the Anglican church, and as you've probably picked up by now, I have some strong opinions on the way they do their ceremonies. I don't let my personal issues stand in the way of the client who wants a religious funeral. But I'm always happy to crash one.

* * *

Mark was a religious man, and knew he would be having a religious funeral. He knew everything that was going to take place except what would happen *after* he took his final breath. He knew I wouldn't deny his dying wish, which was to crash his funeral and read aloud his confession of enjoying an active and social life as a bisexual man. He wasn't shy when talking about his sexual exploits and while most who would attend his funeral already knew about his extracurricular activities, he came from quite a sheltered, religious background, and there were some who had no idea.

Mark engaged the Coffin Confessor for two reasons. Firstly, why not? He thought it a fantastic service. Secondly, he didn't want to put this on any of his family or friends, especially if the church were to call the police. After all, the truth of his sexuality was not something he'd been able to take to the church confessional and share with his priest – his church was very clear on homosexuality, and it would be a major issue to confess in his lifetime. It could well be after his death, depending on how the priest reacted when I began my crash.

I entered the church along with the rest of the mourners and sat in a discreet spot at the edge of the pew, where I could stand up and do my thing without a fuss. All around me were family and friends listening to the priest reading bible quotes and sharing anecdotes

The confessional

about Mark. It was clear the priest didn't know shit about him or his family and friends. The anecdotes were vague and emotionally distant. It was like watching an awkward accountant give a speech at an office party. He even called Mark 'Mike' – not once but twice. It wasn't like Mark was my oldest and dearest friend, but I sure as shit wasn't going to get his name wrong.

The priest asked for those who would like to speak to stand. I stood, but I was going to do more than just speak. I walked towards Mark's coffin, stood before it and turned to the mourners. The priest invited me to the microphone, but I didn't need his invitation, nor did I need a microphone, so I politely rejected his offer and began by announcing my name in a loud, clear voice. I didn't need that introduction either as it turned out. As soon as I started speaking, I heard a lady in the front row whisper to her companion, 'He's the funeral crasher from the news.' I took a quick glance at them and gave a little nod and a smile.

I opened Mark's envelope and began to read. In the letter Mark thanked everyone for being there and assured them that he would miss them as much as they would miss him. He asked those left behind to live a full and loving life, as time is on no man's side. Finally he confessed to loving many women in his lifetime, as well as many men, but at no time had he put himself or others in jeopardy of contracting anything harmful. Mark didn't apologise for his life choices, nor did he ask for forgiveness. While he went to the grave with his fair share of regrets, his sexual preferences weren't among them.

With that, Mark's confession was over. I folded his letter, placed it back in the envelope, put the envelope on the coffin, and walked out, leaving the mourners to digest what I'd just said.

I have no idea if the funeral continued after I crashed it and I don't care. My concern is making sure my clients' last wishes are taken care of regardless of those left behind and any collateral damage that may have been caused. The priest had seemed baffled. In fact, it was like he wasn't sure if I was a friend or foe, but he didn't do anything other than sit there listening while I shared Mark's confession. He didn't try to stop me, which was lucky for him. It was also lucky for the assembled mourners and for Mark, who did not want me to cause harm to his beloved church community.

When I'm engaged to crash a funeral service in a church I'm not arrogant or unnecessarily rude. Well, maybe a little, if the situation calls for it. I generally try to be as respectful as one can be. I let everyone know I'm there on behalf of their loved one and that the deceased invited me. It's not as though I was walking by, saw a funeral and thought I'd crash it for fun. I'm actually there for a reason, a purpose, just like the gathered mourners. The big difference is I was invited and paid far more than the fucking church. But like the church I have a job to do and I'm going to do it. I'm not going to let my personal feelings about organised religion get in the way of that.

* * *

Church isn't a happy place for me. Nor is it a place I would run to for safety, even at my darkest time. While I was a student at the Southport School on the Gold Coast, a school owned and run by the Anglican church, I was repeatedly sexually, physically and mentally abused. One of the teachers told me that because God raped and impregnated a child named Mary – who then gave birth to a bastard son named Jesus – rape was acceptable in the eyes of the Lord. With his interpretation of the bible story, this teacher used God as his excuse to molest, abuse and torment me. While he molested me, he warned me that God sees everything and that if he were doing something wrong God would have punished him. God would punish *me* if I told anyone.

As a child I grew up honestly believing both that God was a rapist and a rape apologist. The teachers taught me that he looked after those who repented and everyone else would burn in hell. So as long as my rapists went to confession on the weekend and confided in the priests who would keep their secret – then God forgave them. It would be me – the victim of abuse, who did not repent – who would end up in hellfire. In the midst of years being raped by religious men in the employ of the church, I was simultaneously forced to attend church and repent my sins. But at age thirteen, I wasn't aware I had any sins, let alone that they needed repenting. I wasn't sure if I should ask God for his forgiveness or why he was ignoring my prayers to stop what I called 'the bad men', the abuse I was suffering at the hands of his representatives.

I don't hate religion because of my upbringing. Nor will I judge another person's beliefs. I just don't believe in any god who would let a child be raped in his own house. I sure as hell don't want that religion rammed down my throat. There may have been a man named Jesus from the Middle East, who may have been a very good and wise man. Just like there was a man named Nelson Mandela from South Africa who was a good and wise man. I'm sure that people may have seen and heard the great things Jesus did and stood for. But I have my doubts and questions about the way his teaching has been interpreted and used as a weapon for thousands of years. Those can't be answered by a man of the cloth or a book that's been rewritten time and time again.

When forced to attend church I would witness the teachers who were abusing me asking for forgiveness, then repeat their sins the following week. This taught me the true meaning of 'repent' as defined by these rapists – to them it meant 'repeat'.

My religion was stolen the same morning my childhood was, and while I can never recover my childhood it was possible to regain my religion. The only problem with that was as each year went by, I wasn't sure which religion to pick and the more I looked into it the more distant I became from it. I grew to hate all things religious; I hated the crucifix, the church and those who worshipped God. When I became a street kid I would break into churches and steal whatever food I could find. Usually this was wine and the pale crackers that I later knew to be communion wafers. Living on the streets I encountered all types of people who would try to recruit street kids to their gangs – but the most common were religious people. I would usually run from them or ignore them, but one afternoon I was approached by two men who said they were born-again Christians.

I didn't know what a 'born-again Christian' was, or what they were talking about. Nor did I care until one of them said they would pay me $10 plus an all-I-could-eat lunch if I'd attend their church service the following morning. There, I was to act as though the demons living inside of me were cast out when their pastor placed his palm on my forehead. Who better to act in front of gullible parishioners than a child who'd had his religion stolen from him and was desperate for food, money and clothing?

The confessional

So I agreed to play the part and the next day I met the two men outside the address they gave me. From the outside it looked like a squash court. That's what the sign on the side of the building said – however it had been turned into a church for those who believed in the born-again. Once inside I was introduced to their priest who handed me two $5 notes and pointed to a table piled high with all types of food and drinks that I could gorge myself on once my act was done.

Prior to my performance one of the men I'd met coached me through my role. While I thought it was funny, he didn't. When I laughed out loud he grabbed me by the hair on the back of my head and hissed, 'Do a good job for the priest, or I'll kick your little arse.' I only laughed harder. Little did he know I'd lived on the streets long enough to know how to fight. If he touched me again, he'd be walking with a limp for the rest of his life. He wasn't that strong, but the rumbling in my belly was, and I gazed longingly at the table laden with the feast and agreed to play along.

Bored, I sat through forty minutes of bullshit, prayer and singing and then finally it was my time to shine. Lining up alongside a number of other parishioners, I wondered if they too were getting paid but none of them fell back the way I was instructed to do. The priest made his way down the line placing his hand on each of our foreheads then pushing us back towards the two men I'd previously met. They would catch us and place us gently on the ground, but when it came for my turn I began to shake uncontrollably, like I was having an epileptic fit.

I guess the parishioners believed that's what demons do – make you act like a fucking nerve case – while the priest placed his hands over my eyes and closed his own, pleading with God to cast out the demons within me. Little did he or anyone else know the demons had been placed there by God-fearing men, so I doubt they were going to be cast out by a God who I'd been taught had wanted me abused and blamed me for it. As far as I understood, the demons were working *for* God, same as the priests.

After the service I made my way to the table laden with food and drink and gorged myself until I was about to throw up. A few parishioners came up and asked if I was okay and if the day's events had taken their toll.

'I feel great,' I said, mumbling the lines I'd been given while eating a handful of chips. 'I've received the Lord's light and am born again.'

The priest and the two men I'd first met thanked me for coming and gave me an extra $5 note. 'We'd love you to come back for next week's service,' they said hopefully.

'No fucking chance.' I didn't want anything to do with them or their fucking church and left hoping never to see either of them again.

But coincidentally, I did. I saw one of them in prison, where he'd just been incarcerated and subsequently bashed by inmates who found out he was doing a stretch for molesting kids. While I didn't do or say anything, I was very happy to see him. Always great to run into old friends in new places.

* * *

So my introduction to religion was complicated, to say the least. It's taken me decades to understand that while I'm not religious

The confessional

I am spiritual and while I don't attend church I have faith and while I don't repent I do ask those I've hurt to forgive me.

I've met all types of people as they are about to exit this world. But they all have one thing in common. When they know they're going to die – atheist and religious alike – they ask God for help and forgiveness. It's like they're hedging their bets.

What I was told about God as a child was abuse on multiple and insidious levels. As was the sexual abuse I suffered. In the years that have passed, I've come to forgive myself, but I'll never forgive those who abused me, nor will I forgive those who stole my childhood and religion. I can only hope if there is a God I'll be forgiven. And honestly, vice versa. If the church really is God's representative on earth, then he has some explaining to do when we finally meet and go toe to toe. And if it happens, the church and I have already gone at least one round.

9

Worse than death

You can't judge a man just by looking at him, but I'm pretty good at getting a handle on people quickly. You need it in my line of work. I definitely needed it back in prison, when getting a read on an individual was often a matter of life or death.

I was first incarcerated when I was just seventeen. I suddenly found myself sharing a shower block with some of the most reviled predators on the planet. You learn to get the measure of a man as soon as he walks into a room, but even so, you never fully know what's going on in someone's head, especially not at first. You have no idea what they do all day, their likes and dislikes, their secrets, what they're hiding in the closet.

I knew little more than the basics about Ben, and he didn't give me a lot of information when he got in touch, other than he needed the Coffin Confessor's services. If I'd known what he wanted ahead of time, I don't know if I would have sat down with him at all. I have an open mind when meeting new clients.

The way I see it, everyone deserves the right to have their final say after their death.

Ben might have been the exception.

We met at his home in Newcastle in mid-2021. He lived in a very nice unit with a view of the ocean on one side and the mountains on the other. It was a home that told you he had a bit of money – I found out his parents had died a decade ago and left him millions. At fifty-seven he was tall, overweight and balding. An ordinary-looking bloke. You'd have a hard time picking him out of a crowd of other generic-looking blokes.

Ben was dying. Not that long ago he'd started getting frequent migraines that would incapacitate him and stop him from doing anything but lie in a dark room. By the time he finally decided to do something about it, it was too late. He had a brain tumour and the cancer had metastasised through his body. Treatment came too late to make any difference, and only made him feel worse. Now he had a full-time carer who I could hear bustling about in the next room, but he seemed cognitively all there, and was able to manage his own affairs. But his time was running out, which was why he called me.

Ben wanted me to deliver a message after he died. Two messages, actually – handwritten letters to his nieces, Louise and Sam, which he put on the table. So far, so good. But I could tell something else was on the way. Something serious. Ben went on to tell me he was a paedophile and a convicted child molester. He'd been charged in the 1990s for touching two little girls – one was his stepdaughter – during a sleepover at his then partner's house. He was given four years, but only served eighteen months. When he got out, he offended again, this time striking closer to home. He said that the letters were to apologise for his acts of paedophilic sexual abuse a decade earlier. He had molested his brother's kids when they were just ten and twelve.

I was taken aback, to say the least. While his crimes had occurred years earlier and he'd done his time for them, that made no difference to me. I saw him for what he was – a putrid grub wearing the skin of a human being. He looked like an ordinary man, but that's how they hide, in plain sight, so that they can perpetrate and get away with their crimes. To be honest, I'd never expected to find myself sitting and listening to the confessions of a paedophile. I guessed he hadn't read my book or done that much research into my background.

Which is odd. You don't have to do much more than google my name to find I'm best known for two things – my career of the Coffin Confessor, and my past as a survivor of child sexual abuse and advocate for other victims. I'd been abused by four grown men – four married, family men who you wouldn't pick out in a crowd – just like this grub. First my own grandfather, and then three teachers at school. One of those teachers was the first person in the world I'd confided in that I'd been molested by my grandfather. When I turned to this bloke for help, his response was to tell me to close his office door. He then proceeded to abuse me while silent tears ran down my cheeks. That day, I changed forever. The trusting little boy who closed the office door was, decades later, still trapped inside me, somewhere deep in my heart. To survive, that boy shut himself off from the world, but in doing so also shut out the joy, the hope, the trust in other people that children are supposed to have. For the rest of my life, I would fight to unmask the paedophiles, rapists and abusers of children, who I consider to be the worst kind of scum on the planet.

And now one of them was sharing his guilt with me and asking for my help.

Whenever I meet a new client, I always keep a professional detachment. It's not easy to shock me, and from the outside, I would have appeared calm as I considered the two envelopes on the table, each addressed simply with a name – 'Louise' and 'Sam'. I doubt Ben noticed my hands shaking as I picked up the letters. In fact, my whole body was shaking. With rage and disgust. And fear. Fear for the little boy who was trapped inside me and who still cried at night, afraid of the predators who stole his childhood. Fear that that little boy, who never found freedom or protection, would be kept safe as my adult personality developed. I evolved from victim to street kid to convict to hard man, finally finding peace with my family. Most of all I feared what I might do to this man if he kept talking about his past.

With a great deal of control, I kept my voice calm and asked him a simple question, one I'd always wanted answered from the men who abused me. 'Why did you do it?'

* * *

While in prison I met some of the worst child abusers on the planet. Not once did I want to sit down and have a conversation with them. I'd learned to respond to any talk or approach from a predator with violence. If an inmate ever showed sexual interest in me, or even disclosed that they had a history of child abuse, my instinct was to start swinging and beat them so badly they'd beg me stop. Within weeks of entering Boggo Road, the whole prison – from the meanest screw to the lowliest rock spider – knew that paedophiles and predators had best steer very fucking clear of me. But there are always exceptions that prove the rule.

The worst of them was Raymond 'Ray' Garland. He was a recidivist rapist and paedophile who had been charged with raping at least three men in prison alone – and each time he had an excuse. It was consensual, but it got a bit rough. Or he was trading sex for protection. I didn't buy it. I'd personally witnessed him physically attack, subdue and drag other prisoners into the toilet block. The screws always looked the other way. Garland had the run of the joint and could go wherever he pleased. It didn't take long to work out that the screws were using him to control inmates that they couldn't control. He was a weapon they could deploy to terrorise any prisoner they couldn't intimidate.

I'd hoped he'd stay away from me, but that wasn't to be the case. I knew one day we would come face to face. He had his reputation and I had mine. The only difference was I wasn't insane, and in a place like Boggo Road, that put me at a disadvantage. And Garland knew it.

We finally went toe to toe one day in the prison yard. I was out for my daily exercise and Garland was walking past the fence line after having his way with yet another young inmate. When I caught his eye, he stopped at the gate of my yard. 'Hey you! Come over here!' he called through the wire fence separating us.

'Fuck off,' I called over my shoulder.

That set him off. He became irate and started yelling and screaming at me that I was dead and that he would have his way with me one way or the other. He even called over the screws to open the gate and when they refused he started to climb the wire fence. I knew he'd never clear the fence, that he was just trying to intimidate me, and I stared at him until he gave up and got down. He started to walk away, yelling over his shoulder that I was dead, and he wouldn't allow this to be the end of it.

But neither would I. 'Hey!' I yelled, walking up to the gate. 'Come back here.'

He did and stopped just on the other side of the wire, so close I could see the whites of his eyes.

'One day soon we're going to be face to face. No fence, no screws,' I said gently. 'And when that happens *you* are going to be the one that dies.'

Garland glared at me. His look was among the most feared in Boggo Road. To be honest it was pretty fearsome. But that's all it was. Just a look. He could see that in my eyes, I was telling the truth. I would do anything to protect the scared little boy inside my heart. And that would have meant grabbing Garland's throat and squeezing until his eyes popped out. And I could see that he could see that.

We stared each other down for a bit longer until he said, 'You're not my type, you got devil in ya.' Then he turned and walked away.

Garland and I never came face to face again. We entered Boggo Road in roughly the same week in 1987, and the cunt is still in there. He's in his early fifties now and has spent just eighteen months of his adult life on the outside. He's still there, still raping boys as they come into the system. At one of his trials for raping another prisoner, he offered the excuse that he himself had been abused when he was eleven, and that was why he had grown up to be a paedophile. He said he enjoyed being abused, so much so that as he grew up, he used to do it to other kids, so they'd have the chance to experience this thing that he'd loved so much.

I don't know. To me that sounds like a fucked-up justification a predator uses to excuse his actions. What goes on inside his mind I'll never know. All I know is that if that fence hadn't been there that day, if we'd been alone for just a minute, then Garland would be dead, and I'd probably still be in prison, still murdering paedophiles.

* * *

Sitting with a paedophile, on a sunny afternoon in Newcastle in 2021, I went into survival mode. Every instinct told me to destroy him. I felt the old rage building inside me, but also, I admit, a bit of curiosity.

When Ben confessed, I was taken aback. At the same time, in a weirdly morbid way, I wanted to hear him out. Part of me needed to understand why. Why had he abused these children? Why did he feel remorse now? Was he born a paedophile, or had he become one because of something that happened to him? Why had he come to me? Instinct was telling me to snap this man's neck and then get the fuck out of there. But another, curious voice was telling me, *No, listen, you might learn something.*

'Why did you do it?' I asked him again. 'Why did you abuse your nieces?'

'I don't know,' he said. 'It just happened.' The answer was disappointing, but I'd known it would be before the words even came out of his mouth. *It just happened.* Thousands of abusers have said as much when they were held to account. This answer, this shrugging off of responsibility – like raping children is something *unlucky* that just happens to some men, like male pattern baldness – is like a fucking reflex for these grubs.

I found meeting Ben extremely confronting. I know I wouldn't want my abuser to track me down and hand me some fucking letter from beyond the grave. I'd rather he just died, painfully, and as far away from me as possible. But the one thing the Coffin Confessor does without question is grant people their dying wish. So I agreed to take the case. At the very least, I figured the victims, his two nieces, deserved some closure.

Ben knew where his brother lived but wasn't sure if his nieces still lived with him given they'd be twenty-one and twenty-three today. Not much to go on, but it was a start. With the letters in hand I got up and started to leave. But I wanted to know one more thing. 'How did you find me, Ben? And what led you to believe that you can trust me to do this for you?'

That's when he smiled, like we were sharing a secret. He told me that he had been following a Facebook page called 'The Lost Boy of TSS', and that he knew I had been sexually abused at the school. 'I'm a former Southport student too. I went to the same school as you. That's why I know I can trust you.'

The penny dropped. Ben had been abused there as a child too. With him, the cycle of abuse had repeated, and he'd become an abuser himself. Which meant he probably assumed that *I* was an abuser too, and so would be a bit softer on him and more inclined to help. This is an assumption, which, I have to admit, didn't help my urge to snap his neck very much. I was careful not to let any emotion show, but something in my expression must have changed, because he seemed suddenly frightened, and understood that our time together was at an end. Letters in hand, I turned my back on Ben the paedophile.

'I'm happy to hear you're being cremated,' I told him as I left. 'My grandfather was buried, and it shits me that he's still around. I guess that's why I visit his gravesite every Father's Day and piss on it.' Then I went home, to my property on the Gold Coast, and filed the letters away, waiting for the inevitable.

On the trip back, I fixated on that moment when I realised that Ben knew that I was an abuse victim, and I saw in his eyes that he knew that I knew. He'd engineered the whole situation, but I didn't understand why. What was he looking for? For me to forgive him? To understand what he'd done? Or to punish him? Was he hoping I'd snap and beat the living shit out of him as some kind of penance? Did he want me to kill him? Maybe he wanted to euthanise himself before he died a painful death alone with his thoughts.

In some ways, I was angrier when he confessed that he knew about my history than I was when he confessed that he was a paedophile. The assumption that came with it – that I would understand the mindset of an abuser – sat uneasily with me. Honestly, it pissed me off.

It's the old story they always used to tell back in the 1960s, 70s and 80s: that if you're abused, you're destined to become an abuser. My own aunty used to say that, and it made my skin crawl. I used to want to punch people in the face for saying that. There was no way that could be an honest explanation. If you went through what I went through, why would you ever want to put that on another person? Especially a child? But you know, a lot of people did, enough that prejudice against survivors of abuse is out there. And when I come up against it, it would be all too easy to blow my top. Like that one time with my cunt neighbour.

* * *

We all have neighbours; some are pleasant, some you just wave to, some annoy us with their loud music, dog barking or weird gardening rituals. I'm incredibly lucky to have landed where I am – living basically in paradise. My property is private, secluded, peaceful and quiet. There's shade for our grandkids to play and fields for our animals to graze. It's far enough from civilisation that when a storm or flood cuts the one road in and out, we're stuck for days to weeks while the damage is repaired. One time a landslide took out a large portion of the road, and I cut my own private track when we needed to get out. But the isolation doesn't worry me. I don't mind being left alone. Like I said, I live in paradise. However . . .

I know this absolute cunt of a person who lives not far from me. An entitled fuck if there ever was one. A weekend warrior who was born rich and never had to work for it. He calls himself an entrepreneur. I call him a drunken fool. I was told a wealthy relative had passed away, leaving a shitload of money that enabled him to purchase the property that he uses as a rally track for his off-road vehicles. He cut pathways through the forest for him and his kids to hoon about on. Which I'm fine with – I've got bikes myself. But I ride them during the day. This neighbour liked to ride at night, after putting away a bit of booze. It usually started around nine and went through to one or two in the morning.

After a few weekends of no sleep thanks to this drunk hooning around in the jungle, I gave him a courtesy call and asked him to tone it down. 'It's a bit loud, mate.'

'Ah, fuck off,' he slurred. 'I'll do what I fucking want.'

I had no problem with him doing what he wanted during the day. But night was a different story. When I let him know it wasn't on, he thought he could abuse and stand me over. But thinking isn't knowing, and I knew how to get him thinking.

So I called the police and made a noise complaint against him for riding his dirt bike at 11:30 p.m.

I've often taken the law into my own hands and used the police to make official complaints that are put on record, in the event I need them down the line. I have a love–hate relationship with the police. In fact I know quite a few that are great people and hate that some officers hide behind the title Police as it just puts all officers, good and bad, in the same basket. Maybe we should start naming the officer who's fucked up and enjoying the luxury of anonymity. Officers aren't supposed to disclose who called them, but this one did, and while I didn't give a fuck if this guy knew or not, it's not for the police to try and escalate the situation. Or is it? I personally believe some officers would rather see a fight or something more serious than a call-out for a noise complaint, but truth be told, some officers wouldn't know what to do and could end up a victim themselves, so it's best they just do their job and not aggravate a problem and come to a sticky end themselves.

Of course, this guy absolutely cracked the shits and next weekend, just as I was lying down to sleep, sure as shit I heard the bikes revving up. That went on for a while, regular as clockwork, him pissed and shooting rifles off into the dark, riding all night, and me calling the cops. Rinse and repeat, until one day it came to a head, and we had it out. As a precaution, because this guy was a pisshead, and things can escalate very quickly when alcohol is involved, I took something with me to record the conversation. Sure enough, when we met just after dark he was already stumbling drunk, a stubby in his hand.

'Mate, you're a fucking idiot,' I said. 'I don't want to put in another complaint, but you're giving me no choice. If you carry on and make noise during the day, I don't give a fuck, but night-time is not on. You're scaring our grandchildren, our horses and the wildlife.'

This set him off.

'Jesus. What the fuck is wrong with you?' I said. I told him I was recording the conversation, but this guy just kept spooling out the rope to hang himself.

'What's wrong with *me*?' he growled. Then he crossed the line. He leered at me and called me a paedophile. This guy said he'd read about me in the news, and that I was sexually abused at The Southport School. He said it was common knowledge that all rape victims turn into abusers themselves, and that he'd warned his kids about me. He'd told them and their friends that I was a paedophile and instructed the kids to call me a pedo to my face and run away. I was gobsmacked.

'Your kids are in fucking primary school and you told them that that's a fucking sensible thing to do? What sort of parenting is that?' I was getting angry now, and I try not to get angry. It's not like I'd never heard this shit before, but the fact he was teaching his kids to be prejudiced against victims of abuse? That was pure evil. Suddenly, I was seconds away from losing control and getting physical. In the moment I was fixated on making this man suffer; he was going to feel a pain like he'd never felt before. But luckily, at the exact same time, he lost his balance, turned, and stumbled off through the darkness. I came to my senses and realised that this pitiful drunk wasn't worth my spending one minute in prison for. Not yet anyway.

I mean it when I say it was a lucky moment. He's lucky he's not eating through a straw for the rest of his life and I'm lucky I'm not doing a life stretch. He must have seen something in my eyes that told him he'd gone too far. The next day he sent me a recorded message saying, 'I'm really sorry, we should talk.' I sent him a text back saying, 'Mate, don't ever come near me. Don't ever look at me. And if I'm in the same restaurant/café/bar you will have to leave.'

And that was it. The bike riding at night is usually done and dusted by 7.30 now, and if it's not I just send a kindly reminder via text. And I've slept like a baby ever since. Best of all, I sleep with a clear conscience, because I resolved the conflict without resorting to violence. It's tempting, and once upon a time I loved nothing more than a good fight – but every time I've done something with violence attached, I always feel the fear afterwards. There's a moment, just a couple of heartbeats between when I hit someone and they hit the ground, when I realise that I might have actually hurt somebody. It happens all the time – somebody gets smacked, they crack their head on the kerb, and suddenly they're dead. That's why I avoid conflict wherever I can. There's a lot of fucking idiots in the world, and if I let myself get frustrated and blow up at the small stuff, it would be carnage.

If someone cuts me off or beeps me in traffic these days, and they start up, I just give them a little friendly little wave to say, 'It would be stupid of me to get out and escalate this, because then you'd be dead, and you don't get to go home to your loved ones tonight, and they would miss you when you're gone, so have nice day.'

Restraint is a professional necessity. If I'd started hitting Ben the paedophile when my gut told me to, for example, he would have ended up dead, one way or another, so I just don't go there. Besides, Ben would soon die on his own, in pain, and alone with his guilt. That's a worse punishment than any I could dish out to him.

* * *

Ben did die and was cremated in November 2021. By then, I'd already found his nieces, Louise and Sam, who were both living in Victoria.

On a Thursday evening shortly after the cremation, I visited the studio apartment where Louise lived. When I rang the doorbell a male in his late twenties answered. Behind him, I could see two women in their early twenties standing around a kitchen bench on which rested four glasses of red wine. The fourth glass belonged to the fourth person in the room – another male, a little older than the rest, and a lot bigger. He was actually massive, with the bulging, puffy look that gym junkies get when they're on steroids. He was a big boy, but I'd seen bigger, and I kept an eye on him anyway. I knew all about how steroids can give you a false sense of power and strength.

'Hello, is Louise home please?' I asked politely.

One of the young women came forward and identified herself as Louise, and asked if she could help me.

'Yes, is that your sister, Sam?' I nodded at the other woman, who was talking to Mr Roid, who now glared at me like he was about to have an attack.

Louise called Sam over and easy as that the two women I had been tasked to track down were now standing in front of me. I explained who I was and what I was doing there. Louise was calm and took her letter to read later. But Sam was more upset. She threw her letter at me, turned and walked towards Mr Roid, who by this stage was striding towards the front door. He grabbed the top of the doorframe, standing behind Louise, and stared at me. I stared right back, because this wasn't a fight, just a staring contest and I'm fucking great at those. I can go all day.

Once upon a time, a client hired me just to stare people down. The client's husband was a degenerate gambler and had lost all their money. The bloke eventually went to jail for stealing from his employer to fund his habit. In the resulting disgrace, the woman's lifelong friends felt embarrassed and abandoned her, judging her silently when she needed their help the most. So she hired me to do the same – to attend her funeral and stand up the back, staring down anyone who dared look at me. Without saying a word, without answering any questions – just staring in intimidating judgement. Dream gig, actually.

So in the scheme of things, Mr Roid was a piece of piss. He was trying to intimidate me when he should have been sizing me up. Judging a person by their physique and demeanour and making assumptions is the best way of losing a fight before it even starts, and I wasn't about to lose this one.

Sensing the situation was escalating, Louise moved to defuse it. 'Thank you,' she said. 'Do you have anything for our father?'

'No, all I have are these two letters,' I replied. I turned my gaze from Mr Roid to Louise and bid her goodnight. With that I was ready to leave but I couldn't help myself. I told Mr Roid that while he thought he was hard, he wasn't. While his physique and glare might intimidate some people, it just gave me a choice: *Take out his knee or his throat?*

As I left I could hear an argument brewing in the background, and I knew Louise and Sam were upset. Not with me, but with their abuser of an uncle, and probably with Mr Roid. I was most pleased with that.

Later on, after filing away my notes on the case, I was talking to my wife about why I'd taken on the job. I'd hoped it would give Ben's two victims some closure, but I still didn't understand why he'd contacted me.

Lara couldn't explain it either. 'If I was a paedophile, the last person on earth I would confide in is you.'

My daughter was more pragmatic. 'Maybe you're the one person left that he *could* talk to about what happened. He needed to reach out to these girls and the only person willing to do the job was you. Maybe he didn't give a fuck about you. Maybe you were just the messenger.'

I want to believe that Louise and Sam were happy their abuser was dead, and that his final days were full of pain and remorse. That there was some solace in that for them. But it's a strange thing – abuse affects people in different ways. And you could tell one of the victims was a survivor. Louise wasn't a victim. She was strong and had moved on. Sam was more in need of help. You don't have a guy like Mr Roid hanging around because you've achieved inner peace. Choosing a bloke like that suggested her days and nights were still tarnished by visions of abuse. Every survivor deals with their trauma differently and I've been some version of both of those girls at different stages of my life.

With Lara's help, I've come a long way in how I process my abuse. These days my past is a source of strength – fuel to power me towards a better life. It wasn't always that way, though. Once upon a time, the only thing I wanted was to die, and to take revenge on my abusers before I went. Which was how I ended up in the Southport School clock tower.

* * *

When I was a kid, I got very close to attempting what would have been Australia's first mass school shooting. I didn't know how to deal what had happened to me in a healthy way. It speaks to the fucked-up state of my mind back then that the best option I could hit upon was to confront my abusers and gun them down.

This was around 1985. I was a street kid on the Gold Coast, sleeping rough – in movie theatres when I could, and sometimes in boats moored on the Broadwater by rich folks who barely ever used them. I knew which boats were rarely attended and were safe for me to crash in. This was before going to prison. I'd dropped out of school to get away from the predator teachers, but I couldn't get them out of my head. I fantasised about revenge, day and night.

The Boomtown Rats' song 'I Don't Like Mondays' was all over the radio that year. It seemed to be following me around. I'd hear it playing in the alleyway behind the bakery where I'd scavenge meals, in the lobby of the cinema I shared with the rats at night, and from the radios of cars driving up and down the avenue. The song's lyric is about a teenager who snaps, takes a gun to school, and mows down her teachers and classmates. It's a weird song, because it's pretty upbeat and happy considering it's about shooting people. The band's singer, Bob Geldof, made it sound like that was a perfectly reasonable solution to my problems. To my ears, it seemed to make sense.

It was a terrible, terrible time for me. Life was a vicious cocktail. I was living a precarious existence within spitting distance of the school where my abuse took place, my mental health was as fucked as it had ever been, and I had access to guns. Guns were much more readily available back then – every second family home had a rifle. I got my hands on a Winchester .22 rifle that I stole from my mate's dad, who was an avid shooter. It was a beautiful gun, oiled wood, gold-plated, the poor guy's pride and joy. But I nicked it, along with a box of ammunition, and stashed it all in a boat on the Broadwater where I sometimes slept, knowing it wouldn't be found.

There I'd sit for hours, lost in visions of taking the gun to the school and hunting down the men who'd abused me. I fixated on the clock tower – this huge, elegant edifice attached to a building in the middle of the campus that was the school's pride and joy. I imagined climbing up into it, setting up a little sniper's crow's nest, and shooting the people who'd hurt me, one by one. I'd already left school by this stage, and was yet to go to jail, but that was probably the most dangerous I'd ever been in my life. Just a scared, skinny kid with no reason to live except a desire to kill. I'd sit there and fantasise about shooting those teachers, seeing their brains splattered over the spotless courtyards and manicured lawns of their precious school.

Realistically, I probably couldn't have done much with a .22 rifle from that height. I wasn't an expert shot, and this is a gun designed for hunting rabbits and maybe deer in the bush. Not fragging paedophiles from a clock tower 15 metres up in the air. The most likely outcome would be that the cops would come for me, and I would jump to my death. Unless I was lucky enough that they gunned me down and saved me the trouble. At that point, life wasn't worth living. I didn't care whether I lived or died. To be honest, I didn't think I was going to come out of that clock tower alive.

It wasn't a big deal. My thinking was all over the shop. I'd only just met Lara and although we'd hit it off I didn't know we were going to become an item. So I didn't feel I had anything to live for. I wasn't very strong back then and it seemed like a good way to die. I'd come close to leaping off a building a couple of times before, but I'd never gone through with it. I was suicidal, but the thought of shooting myself never crossed my mind. I stole the gun for revenge, to inflict violence on the men who had hurt me. That's what a gun is for, violence, and revenge was my motive. So to end my life before that was not what I wanted. I wanted to die, but not until I'd had my vengeance.

I came very close. I'd snuck into that clock tower quite a few times to plan it all out. Really, it was a flip of a coin whether one day I'd climb up there and start murdering people, or whether I'd just go and scavenge some dinner from the bin behind the bakery. In the end I chose dinner, and before I changed my mind I threw the gun into the Broadwater. It's probably still there to this day, rusting in the mud.

I still sometimes wonder, *Why didn't I go ahead with it? What stopped me?* I think my logical side won out. The realisation of not being able to shoot the actual teachers from the clock tower was one factor. I imagined how fucked I would feel if I got up there and wasn't able to actually hit the right people. But the main factor was the collateral damage it would have caused. I thought of all the innocent kids just wandering around the school, worried about their maths grades, or that they'd be dropped from the rugby team, or getting a date to the school formal, or whatever it was kids living a normal childhood worried about. I imagined those kids getting caught in the crossfire, or me accidentally hitting one, and just how traumatic it would be if gunfire started ringing out in the middle of the school day. In the end, that's what brought me back and pulled me off that road of violent vengeance. Why hurt people who'd never hurt me? It wasn't worth ruining the life of some innocent kid just to satisfy my bloodlust. I wanted justice for the abuse I'd suffered, but I'd have to find another way of getting it.

* * *

For much of my life, I thought that I was the only one who'd suffered at the hands of the paedophiles at my school. Far from it. The predators abused countless boys over the years. My eyes were truly opened when the Southport old boy and sports legend Peter 'Jacko' Jackson closed his eyes for the last time. Jacko was a successful and popular rugby league player in the 1980s and 90s. Peter was also a police officer. From the outside, he was every bit the Aussie success story: great career, beautiful wife, three young kids, happy life. But in 1997 he died of a heroin overdose. In the aftermath of his death, the world found out he'd been struggling with the abuse he'd suffered from his house master and footy coach at the Southport School. It had broken him and finally led to his early death.

That was the moment I knew I wasn't alone. If there were two of us, and this guy was a massive success in every way and was too ashamed to speak for years and years, then there were bound to be others in our situation. So I went public. I started speaking out about the abuse I'd suffered. I named and shamed my abusers, because that is the only thing these monsters are truly scared of. The truth. I did this knowing full well that they'd take legal action. The Southport School and the Anglican church, who owned the school, were going to throw me to the wall, and my name and finances would be dragged through the mud. Lara knew it too but had my back every step of the way.

'We're going to lose everything,' I told her.

'I know. So be it,' she said.

'Are you sure you're with me on this?'

'I'm sure. You're taking a chance, but I also know there's no chance you're going to back down. So I'm with you all the way.'

I went to the police, who did fuck all, and to the media, who ignored me, but the litigation from the school and church came rolling in anyway. It carried on like that until around

2010, when in response to the church's attempts to silence me, I started a Facebook page called 'The Lost Boy of TSS'. It began with a single post detailing my abuse. I said that the police knew everything, that the church knows about and protects abusers, and that the Southport School knows what happens under their roof.

The school immediately tried to get the post taken down, but by then it couldn't be stopped. It had started an avalanche. Boys who'd been abused at the school told their stories. Teachers who'd turned a blind eye to the abuse told theirs. All of a sudden I had momentum, and the church finally came to the table. Even if they had to be dragged there. For the next ten years, representatives of the school painted me every shade of shit you can imagine. I was threatened legally, physically, emotionally, and called a liar more times than I can remember.

At first, they tried to use my past against me, suggesting my criminal record and difficult early life proved that I was untrustworthy. The lawyers tried to spin the facts – that I had been a street kid, then a prisoner who struggled with mental health – and that this was proof I *wasn't* abused, rather than it being the consequences of abuse. But I never took a backward step. After a shit childhood, and with Lara's help, I had learned to use the abuse to better my life, not let it control or define me.

That upset the church's lawyers more than anything else I did. Their playbook when confronted with allegations of abuse is to find the weakest link – the people who were broken by their abuse in childhood, rather than hardened – and force a paltry settlement. They prey on the people still struggling with mental illness or addiction and offer them some pathetic amount of money in exchange for their silence. This sets a precedent, encouraging others to sweep it all under the rug. It allows the powers that be to quietly move paedophiles on and continue their abuse.

The owners of the Southport School, the Anglican church, have recently paid out a number of victims I've assisted, and while I'm delighted they're being compensated for the abuse they suffered I'm deeply concerned and pissed off that the perpetrators get to walk free. It's all about money, for the church. Nothing more, nothing less. They have conditioned the public to view victims as drug addicts and drunks – the dregs and outcasts of society. When confronted with someone who refuses to quietly wear those labels – who has more courage, strength and determination than most – they lose their main defence. They panic and try to conjure up some bullshit they hope will stick.

From around the age of thirteen, I kept a diary. By the time the church finally had to face up to what they'd put me through, I'd accumulated forty-two volumes. Most were unreadable due to my dyslexia, but I knew what was on each and every page. Now the church does too, along with their small army of lawyers. In an effort to discredit me, they demanded my childhood diaries be presented as evidence. I handed them over, but found the process to be an invasion of my privacy on a level I'd only ever experienced when being sexually abused. After the diaries came back from the church's lawyers, I incinerated every last one of them. I've since given up the habit.

As part of the legal shit-slinging, in 2021 I met with Dr Malcolm Foxtrot, a prominent and renowned psychiatrist. He asked about my time in Boggo Road Gaol, in order to ascertain how it had affected me.

'Truth be told, I wasn't affected, I was educated,' I told him, sharing some of my stories. When I mentioned the name Ray Garland, Dr Foxtrot's face went pale and his voice started to shake. He said he had worked in the prison system for a long time, and counselled a number of men who were raped and brutalised by Garland. I can't say I was surprised. But I think I surprised him with my story. The psychiatrist verified that I was an honest and credible abuse survivor. It was his professional opinion, delivered in a six-page report, that helped me to get the church to agree to settle. For a while there, they switched tactics. They said the fact I went from a homeless convict to find success in several careers and enjoyed a level of financial comfort was proof that I hadn't been abused. They said this proved I wasn't a typical victim. But finally, after years of dodging their responsibilities, they agreed to pay 'mediated damages' for the abuse I'd suffered in their institutions.

The mediation was set for early September 2023 – by chance, the day after Lara's birthday. So we decided to make the most of it. We arrived in the city the day before, checked into a nice hotel, and went out for a beautiful birthday dinner to celebrate Lara. We sat across from each other, holding hands, and I felt very deeply the years between us in which she'd been by my side every step of the way. The next day would hopefully conclude a fight we'd been fighting together for over two decades. And here we were. With not much more than the love and strength we'd given each other, we were close to achieving the impossible.

It was the morning of the mediation, and I hadn't slept a wink. Lara on the other hand was exhausted given we'd spent the previous day eating, drinking, celebrating her birthday and exploring Brisbane. I'd also treated her to a spa pampering package. As for me, I was constantly thinking of the mediation. I couldn't ignore the fact that it was either going to end a decades-long fight, or see me dragged further through the justice system. As a victim of that system, I have little to no respect for it, given how many child abuse perpetrators get off or receive a far less onerous sentence than those who steal money. I once heard a father of a victim yell out in a courtroom, 'You can steal our children but don't dare touch our money.' It's a statement I found true within the justice system.

As Lara lay comfortably asleep, I decided to go for a walk. It was about 4.30 a.m., and as I exited the hotel I could see a street sweeper and a delivery truck making its rounds, dropping off fruit and vegetables at the doorways of cafés and restaurants.

I didn't know which way I was going to walk – and to be honest I didn't care. I was just happy to be doing something other than thinking about what the day might bring. But that didn't last long. As I walked, I started to think more, especially about the things that could go wrong, given I had very little trust in my legal team.

I was a constant pain in the arse for them. They wanted nothing more than for me to settle. It was as if they were terrified of going to court. I realised after some time that their business model – 'no win, no fee' – was solely based on settlements. Nothing more, nothing less. I felt that going to court terrified them, but what terrified them *more* was confronting the church. And the church and their lawyers knew it.

The sun was just rising and I could see glimpses of its rays between the city's tall buildings. It's a city I was once incarcerated in – a city I neither hate nor love, but one I find different to others I've visited.

Brisbane is notorious for its seedy night clubs, underground casinos and sex clubs, probably nothing dissimilar to most major cities. But not all cities had the Fitzgerald Inquiry into police and political corruption, or the Whiskey Au Go Go nightclub fire-bombing, or Boggo Road Gaol.

As I walked, I could literally see the dawn of a new day, and more activity around me. While I'm not what you call a 'people person', when I passed someone walking their dogs they'd get a smile or a good morning from me. I've always had this silly belief that I only have so many smiles, and I don't like to give them all away to strangers.

As I thought about the possibility of being dragged through court or sued – or even arrested – I came across a number of people sleeping on the street. I recognised the smell – a smell that's not easily forgotten, a smell that wrenched me back to when I was a street kid myself, living rough with more troubles than I was facing at this present moment. It was this realisation that snapped me out of the depressing dead-end I'd found myself walking towards. I turned around, took a deep breath of that ungodly smell of hurt and isolation, and headed back towards Lara, still fast asleep in the hotel room.

I looked around at all the things I'd just passed with a different perspective. My pace was more assured, and I felt calmer, my breathing easier. I thought how a city can swallow you up if you let it, or it can embrace you and allow you to explore it. I chose the second option.

Lara had no idea that I'd slipped out for a walk, or that I'd just received a dose of wake-the-fuck-up-Bill.

We went for breakfast at an eatery along the riverbank – a

beautiful spot. Lara was concerned about the mediation, but I assured her that all was well. By the day's end we would be embracing each other like never before, and she'd be free of the ongoing burden of a husband's plight to seek justice. And I would have the freedom I'd been wanting since my eighth birthday.

It was time for me to attend the mediation, and as I said goodbye Lara gave me a hug. She told me that no matter what happened she would always support and love me, and with that I left.

The mediation took place in one of the towering buildings that circled the city, and even though we were on a high floor we couldn't see out of the windows. Maybe this was for distraction or intimidation purposes, just like the placement of the chairs around a large table that could easily sit twenty people. My chair was strategically placed so that I was front and centre.

It's better for one's health and pocket not to disclose what occurs during mediation. I focused my thoughts on Lara and the family we had built around us, all things beautiful.

And then it was done. In the end, I accepted a settlement – not for me but for Lara, my children and my grandchildren. I was free from my long fight for justice, one that had taken twenty-five years, six lawyers and thousands in legal fees, but I'd won. I'd dragged the giants I'd been fighting my whole life to the table, to finally meditate on what had been done to the boy I'd been.

To be honest, I don't feel like I received justice. In a just world, the men who abused me would be in prison. Instead, they were allowed to walk free. They'd lived easy lives, protected by the school and the church, and were now elderly and frail. They should rot in prison. But soon enough, they'll be burning in hell. Not that I believe in hell, but the church sure does and it's coming for them. But the terms of the settlement mean I can't go after the church or my abusers anymore – so justice wasn't delivered.

So I didn't get justice, but I did get revenge.

I felt satisfaction in knowing that I had kicked the fucking doors in of a privileged private school and exposed the sexual, physical and mental abuse bestowed upon the children in their care. I found solace in knowing that students today are better protected, and relief in knowing that because of my actions victims who once suffered in silence are now survivors who have found their voice.

I left 'The Lost Boy of TSS' Facebook page up. I've stepped away from it for the most part, but I maintain it so that other survivors can rally and support each other. Because that's how the healing starts for many of us.

The money is neither here nor there after a lifetime of suffering. The more valuable thing was the acknowledgement implicit in the payout. The fact they came to the table means they know they had wronged me, and despite their best attempts to destroy me, they'd failed. For me it was closure. Or was it?

After walking away from the mediation I felt something I hadn't expected. Alone. I'd imagined this moment many times over the years, and thought that I'd feel triumphant, or victorious, or angry, or relieved. There was none of that. Just the feeling of being alone, in a way I hadn't felt since I was a little boy, when I was first abused by an adult predator. I was on the verge of what I thought was a panic attack, and suddenly I had to get off the street. Quickly, I walked into some random clothes store, grabbed a jumper off the rack, walked into the dressing room and pulled the door closed behind me. There, holding this jumper, staring at myself in the mirror, I felt part of myself leave. The little boy who I'd locked away and had been carrying with me since he was first betrayed by his grandfather, who I'd kept protected in my heart through years and years of fighting and violence and pain – that little boy was speaking to me. And he was ready to go.

It wasn't my decision to let him go. He wanted to go. If I had a choice I would have wound back that moment and kept him with me. But it wasn't up to me. He'd brought me here to say goodbye. It was time for me to live my own life. That's why I felt alone. Because that little boy, and all the trauma he'd felt, had been my companion in life. Which didn't make sense because of course I wasn't alone. When I walked out of that dressing room, I would go home to Lara, my two children and my six grandchildren. But the little boy who I'd once been was at peace now, and it was time for him to be put to rest, and for me to live a life without him. *Really* live. With all the joy and euphoria and excitement and fear that I'd never properly let in, because I had that boy to protect. Now, in that dressing room, crying into a jumper, my life was beginning.

This is the part I was unprepared for, that every survivor who reads this needs to know. *That it's worth the fight.* That when everything is resolved, and you've come to terms with your survival, you can finally move on. It wasn't my choice, I didn't realise it was going to happen, but it was happening. I should have anticipated it, but after all the fighting is done, there's peace. *And it's worth it.*

In the face of evil, I yelled, kicked and screamed, I refused to remain silent, and I exposed those who sexually, physically and emotionally hurt the little boy within. But now it was time to say goodbye. As I said these words, I composed myself and left the dressing room knowing I would be okay. Life as I knew it was about to change for the better.

10

Die living

Vengeance is pretty hollow. Most of the time. But sometimes, it's exactly what you need for closure.

On Christmas Eve 2022, I was spending the night with the family. My wife, our two kids, and our six grandkids, all under four, who call me by the same nickname: 'Popeye'. Late that night, after almost everyone was in bed, I received a lengthy text from a woman named Monica. Monica was from Maitland, New South Wales, a town I knew little about, except that it was rough. Maitland Gaol was as notorious a hellhole as Boggo Road back in the day. When I was serving time as a teenager I would often meet other prisoners from across the country, and the guys coming from Maitland were among the hardest. The reported assault rate in Maitland Gaol was *ten times* the state average. A tough place, and fair to say Monica from Maitland was coming out of the gate pretty hot.

'Hello, I hope this message is not ignored but I'll understand if you disregard it given what this day means to so many.' The text went on to explain that she'd read about me and my work and wanted to discuss a matter close to her heart. 'There's a person in my life that I'd like to see tormented after my death and I believe you're just the man I'm looking for. Can you please reply with a number I can call. If I don't get a reply I'll know that you're just another fraudster.'

I took a minute to decode all this. This woman was clearly emotional. But emotions run high at Christmas, especially for those who share their lives with ghosts. At first impression, Monica was also bitter. Maybe she'd reached out to others for help and had been let down before. Hers was a pretty familiar request. A lot of people's last wish is to inflict pain on others. I get it. I've been lucky enough to find closure, but for some people who've been badly hurt, vengeance seems like their only option.

But on Christmas Eve? The way I saw it someone had to have fucked this lady over in a very profound way for her thoughts to be about causing torment on Christmas Eve. Then again, I got it. There's no lonelier night of the year than Christmas Eve if your only company are your demons. Back in the day, Christmas Eve was a night for quiet reflection and prayer with the family. Go back in further in history, and this time of year was known as a night when ghosts came to visit you. It's no coincidence that *A Christmas Carol* happens on Christmas. Monica was clearly haunted by something.

Re-reading her text I thought of all those people who fear this time of year – who don't see it as a time of enjoyment but dread it as a day of sorrow. I looked up from the phone and at the family Lara and I had created and couldn't help but feel blessed and thankful. Part of that was understanding how it would feel *not* to have that feeling. I knew I had to reply to Monica if only to let her know she had been heard.

'Hello Monica, I can't imagine what this time of year means to you given you're texting me on Christmas Eve but know that I have read it and will be more than happy to assist you, the Coffin Confessor.'

* * *

Christmas came and went, Boxing Day too by the time Monica replied on 29 December. She apologised for contacting me on Christmas Eve and asked if I had time to call her. I did so immediately. Over the phone she was very polite. She had the voice of an older lady with a broad Aussie accent but old-fashioned good manners. She again apologised for contacting me on Christmas Eve, but I reassured her there was nothing to apologise for and asked how I might help her. Monica's story was sad, even by the standards I regularly came across in my line of work. She had survived the loss of her daughter, Merry, while she was young, and then the loss of her husband, Anton, who had taken his own life. Anton lived with a heavy heart after losing Merry and decided to be with her in the afterlife. He left Monica a note telling her he loved her deeply and that she would be well provided for, but that he needed to be with Merry. Monica understood. She had never felt anger towards Anton over his decision – in fact, she loved him even more for wanting to be with their daughter.

For her part, Monica had gone on living, although cancer had tried to take her twice. She fought back both times, however she'd recently been diagnosed for the third time, and on this occasion she would allow it to end her life. She explained she'd been in and out of hospital the past year and had decided to die at home surrounded by her treasured garden. She was fortunate to have been provided for by her late husband and took nothing for granted, and had already written her will deciding who would benefit from her death. And who would suffer from it. Which is why she called me.

During the phone call we arranged to meet face to face in the second week of the new year 2023 in her hometown of Maitland.

As I arrived at Monica's home I noticed two cars. One was a white practical Toyota 4WD and the other a red electric piece of shit. Before I could get to the door a woman in her fifties opened it and introduced herself as Monica's home helper. She told me that Monica was really looking forward to meeting me. 'She's been reading about you on her iPad for weeks. I haven't seen her so enthusiastic about anything for ages.'

I was shown to Monica's bedroom. She seemed energised and full of life. If it weren't for the hospital bed and life-support equipment surrounding it, I wouldn't have thought she was close to death. Monica was in her late seventies. She had thick brown hair – that she later revealed was a wig – and a smile that couldn't be faked. You could tell by the lines on her face that she had lived, laughed, loved and lost.

'So you *are* real,' she laughed. 'Not a fraudster and obviously don't scare easily! Come in, sit down. You look as handsome in real life as you do on my iPad.'

Monica got right to the point. She wanted me to help provide closure for her daughter, Merry, who'd been killed riding on the back of a motorbike her abusive boyfriend, Blake, was driving while drunk. Blake had threatened Merry that if she didn't ride home with him, he'd bash her father, Monica's late husband, Anton. Merry took the threat seriously – Blake and Anton had come to blows previously, with Anton coming off second best.

Sure enough, on the way home, Blake lost control of the bike and the ensuing accident took Merry's life. Blake got off with little more than a broken foot and a few scratches. On top of that, he blamed Merry for the crash – saying she was trying to jump off every time he slowed the bike and that's why he'd stacked it. Blake was full of bile about it, and tormented Monica and Anton any time he saw them. He would spit in their direction and call them fucking dogs. After Monica's husband took his own life, Blake called Monica to tell her that her recently deceased husband was a gutless pig.

Monica's request was a face-to-face confrontation with Blake to pass on a simple message: that in death she would hunt down every person he'd ever loved and lost until such time as he himself died. She wanted Blake to know he would be haunted and tormented and that she would do everything possible to make what life he had left miserable. Regardless of whether he believed in God, heaven, hell or the afterlife, Monica would find a way to come back and make him suffer.

Straightforward. Something I was happy to do. The only issue was she wanted the message delivered while she was still alive, and she wanted it recorded so she could see the look on Blake's face. That way, she would have some satisfaction prior to joining Anton and Merry.

Monica gave me Blake's last known home and workplace addresses, which was more than I needed to track him down. I told her I'd be back in a few days. As I said my goodbyes, there was one thing I was still curious about. 'Why did you reach out to me on Christmas Eve? Of all nights?'

'That was our daughter's birthday,' Monica said. 'That's why we called her Merry.' Each year of Merry's life, the family had celebrated her birthday the night before Christmas, until Blake's actions ended it all.

For once in my life, I didn't have anything to say. I didn't need words though. Instead, I held Monica's hand. She could see in my eyes that I understood. I had a busy schedule, it was the holiday season, but fuck waiting – I would find this shitbag and do this job immediately. It took me all of five minutes to track Blake down. But first I needed to compose myself. I wanted to make sure I didn't escalate the situation more than was appropriate. I needed a feed too, so I found a pub and had a steak lunch followed by a nip of port.

As I left the pub I put Blake's address into my phone and navigated past a row of shops, to a suburban street. The target destination held twin duplexes – on the right-hand side was a manicured garden and a neatly mown lawn. The property on the left was derelict – dirt and weeds with an old car on blocks surrounded by scrap metal. Years of experience as a private investigator had me assuming that Blake lived in the hovel, but no, the satnav insisted he was in the lovely home on the right. A bit of a conundrum. GPS navigation can get it wrong sometimes, and I didn't want to go kicking in the wrong door. So I sat in the car for a moment, deciding on a plan of action, until I noticed an elderly woman leaving from the home on the left. I approached her.

'Excuse me, but I'm looking for a man named Blake. Does he live around here?'

'He does. That arsehole lives next door. He plays his music at all hours of the day and night. He has no respect.' She told me Blake lived alone – he'd had a girlfriend, but she'd moved out two weeks ago, around Christmas time, taking their son with her. Prior to that, the police were always coming around. Along with the kid, the girlfriend had taken the car, so now Blake came and went on his motorbike at all hours, waking her up.

This was a lot of information. Getting info out of people is something I've always been good at – as you know, I have one of those faces – which made me a good PI, but I barely had to ask a question. This woman clearly needed to vent about her prick of a neighbour. I thanked her and she didn't ask who I was or where I was from, only that, 'You're better off not knowing Blake. He's no good.' With that she left, walking up the street towards the shops.

I was just turning to leave when I heard a motorbike approaching in the distance. It pulled up and, from Monica's description, I could easily identify the guy who climbed off it. Blake was in his fifties or maybe late forties with a lot of city miles on the clock. He was a heavily built guy, a bit overweight with muscles turning to fat. About five foot ten, balding with a few tattoos on his head to make up for where his hairline was running away from him. A mean-looking bastard, who'd dropped right into my lap. Sometimes these things just happen. Call it fate or coincidence. Or maybe a Christmas miracle.

He climbed up the stairs to the front door of the duplex. I waited a good ten minutes before I made my approach. I strapped a body camera to my jacket to record the interaction and started up the flights of steps to Blake's front door. I could hear music blasting from inside. 'Another Brick in the Wall' by Pink Floyd. Now I was in an even worse mood. That song always resonated with me, the chorus about teachers who wouldn't leave kids alone. Blake couldn't have known how much that song pissed me off, but there you go. Another Christmas miracle. Through the window I could see him in the lounge room sitting in a massage recliner. When I knocked he seemed visibly pissed off that he had to get up and answer the door. He didn't cheer up when he opened it and saw me standing there.

'What the fuck do you want?' he asked, warily. He probably thought I was police or some kind of detective due to the way I was dressed and with my body cam pointed in his direction. He was even uglier up close and clearly wasn't winning any prizes for personality either. My guess is he enjoyed scaring people like that poor little old lady next door. But he was shit out of luck now, trying to stare me down.

'Blake, I'm the Coffin Confessor,' I said. 'I have a message for you from Monica.'

'Oh yeah? I've heard of you,' he spat. 'And you're not shit. Neither is that fucking pig old lady. Tell her to shove her message up her arse.'

I wouldn't be doing that, but I did have to deliver the message, so ended up force-feeding it to him. He was going to get the memo one way or the other, and while it took a little persuasion, he heard it, fully digested it, thought about his actions, and apologised to Monica. He meant it too. So I'd done my job and while I may have gone a little too far it wasn't far enough for a prick like Blake. That said, I'm pretty good at control. I know how to keep a situation in hand, I know what I'm capable of, and I know the dangers of overstepping the fine line I walk most days.

When faced with a little opposition, Blake was as fake as the cheap prison-grade tats running up his neck. It's the weaklings who dress up as hard cunts and make victims of the women in their lives. And this was a prime example of a 24-carat weak cunt. I took care to remind him to respect the women and elders in his life before I let him go.

As I left Blake's place the elderly woman I met earlier waved at me on her way back from the shops. I could only hope Blake honoured his promise of respecting her.

* * *

Back at Monica's place I was greeted by her nurse. 'Hello,' she said. 'I hope you have good news. She's in great spirits today.' The nurse made me a coffee and a pot of herbal tea for Monica and escorted me to Monica's bedroom, making sure she was dressed and composed before I entered.

Monica explained that while she understood the nurse had to come and go all the time, the treatment was harsh and she wished it would end soon. She said this with sincerity and a smile. As soon as the nurse left the room I told Monica that her wishes had been granted and that Blake had received her message loud and clear. I showed her the video and she smiled with the brightest, most satisfied grin I've ever seen. It got bigger and bigger the more the video went on, and the louder Blake begged and cried.

'Thank you,' she said, simply. 'Thank you.'

'You're welcome,' I said. I then offered her a gift – to download the video onto her phone so she could watch it whenever she liked.

'That's sweet. But if the wrong person found it after I died, I wouldn't want you to get in trouble. You go ahead and delete it.'

This was something I'd considered, but didn't want to trouble Monica with. I was grateful that she cared enough to make sure I was safe. Then, with our Christmas gifts exchanged, we said goodbye forever.

On the drive back to the Gold Coast, I reflected on the case, and how lucky I was to have ended up with a life where, despite every cunt and evildoer I've had to deal with, I'm so happy. I could have so easily wound up with a situation like Monica's – where she'd been so badly fucked over that her only solace was to cause another human being pain.

I wondered if there was anyone out there who hated me so much that they would want to come back and haunt me. It occurred to me that I know more people who are dead than I do alive and wondered if any of them were ever going to come and visit me with a 'Good job, well done', or perhaps some tips about the afterlife, 'Make sure you do this before you travel'.

It may be surprising that I'm not a vindictive, bitter, unhappy person after all that I've been through. But I'm not, thanks to the one big miracle of my life. The one that brought all the other miracles with it. Meeting Lara, and starting our family, and all the joy of a loving home, which I was now driving back to. Maitland, like Boggo, like all the trauma of the past, was firmly in the rear-view mirror.

* * *

That Christmas I realised that, after everything, I was finally through all the pain. For the longest time, pain was my friend. It was a way for me to feel something. But now, between letting go of the traumatised child inside my heart and having my grandkids fill the space he'd once lived in – I didn't need pain in my life anymore.

Years ago I would hurt myself deliberately. I sought out violence and scratched that itch by working as a bouncer. When you're at the door of a nightclub in Queensland, there'll always be some kind soul who's willing to give you a good smack in the head.

I sometimes still need to feel pain just to know that I'm alive. Just recently, I went to the dentist. I had seven silver fillings and they needed updating. Lara and I have been going to this dentist every year for years, so I told the dentist what I wanted: all seven fillings removed, properly drilled out, and replaced with porcelain. She said that wouldn't be a problem, told me how much it would cost, and booked me an appointment two days later. When I arrived for the appointment I jumped in the chair like it was a roller-coaster. I couldn't wait.

'Alright, I want you to do all seven, today,' I said. 'With no anaesthetic, please.'

'I . . .' She looked at the dental nurse to check she'd heard right. 'I can't do that.'

'Why not?' I asked.

'We've never done that before.'

'First time for everything.'

'Are you sure?'

'If it goes bad, we'll work it out. If it goes well, I'll put you in my next book. Whatever, let's go.'

So she went in, no anaesthetic, no nothing. Three and a half hours later it was done. After heaps of drilling, blood everywhere, tears in my eyes; I had the time of my life.

'How do you feel?' the dentist asked me, taking my glasses and the bib.

'I feel good,' I said. I really did.

Sometimes I need to go down that rabbit hole. Once in a while I get the urge to experience some real pain as a kind of circuit breaker, but a quick visit to the dentist will fix that. It's important to look after your dental health, especially when you're getting on in years. But those times when I seek out pain happen less and less often nowadays. Since the grandkids have come along, my relationship with pain has changed. If I'm ever going down that dark mental path, all I have to do is look at those kids and I feel good again. They changed everything. I look at them and I think I don't need to be in pain. I had that realisation a couple of months ago. I was like, *Wait a minute, what's going on? Why do I feel like this? Why do I feel so good? Why do I feel . . . happy?* Family. Simple as that.

* * *

The following Christmas we took a holiday to the beach. Me and Lara, my kids and all six of my grandchildren. We went to a nice resort and we stayed there for the Christmas period, most of which I spent swimming and building sandcastles.

Life has a way of putting your experience into perspective, if you give it long enough. There was a time I was so fucked up that if I saw an old man playing innocently with children at the park or the beach, I'd be filled with rage. I couldn't see any grandfather as anything but a shadow of the man who'd physically and mentally abused me. I never thought it would be otherwise. But here I was, a 55-year-old splashing about, running and tumbling with my six grandchildren all under the age of five, not giving it a second thought.

Once upon a time, I would have felt self-conscious spending time alone with a child. If I took my kids to the park, I'd want Lara by my side so that everyone would know that I had a good reason to be there. How fucked up is that? I had no idea how fucked up it was until I didn't think that way anymore. At last I could watch all the other grandads on the beach, playing with their families, and I could wave at them, because that's how life is supposed to be.

For the first time in my fifty-five years I'd come to the realisation that not everyone was out to get me, hurt me or see me fail. It's only now I look back with sadness and see how many opportunities I've wasted in not having long and loving friendships. It took my family for me to see that. They have a way of teaching me that lesson, every time I need reminding.

One day during that beach holiday, I went for a swim. When I came back to the house, the family, unbeknown to me, decided to prank me. They were going to pretend I was dead. They'd talk to each other, but not recognise me. I walked in the door and everyone ignored me. Then my son kicked it off, 'I thought I felt a breeze. Is there a draught in here?'

My daughter then chipped in, 'Oh, did you hear that? I thought I heard Dad!'

'No, he's been gone a while now,' someone else said. 'Don't you miss him?'

Then my three-and-a-half-year-old grandson piped up, 'Where did Popeye go?' I don't know how a toddler gets to be such a good actor. He should have got an Oscar for that performance. For a second I almost believed he really couldn't see me, and I was a fucking ghost. This scenario went on for ages. They just kept on doing it. And at first it was funny. And then I thought it was *very* funny, but then I got a bit frustrated. Then I got angry. Then I got upset. *What the fuck are you talking about?* I wanted to ask, but couldn't swear in front of the grandkids, so instead I said, 'I'm right here!'

'Oh, weird,' my daughter said. 'I just got chills up my spine like someone else was right here, now, in the room with us.'

'Alright then, enough of this, I'm grabbing the port,' I said, going for the bottle we'd bought for the holiday.

At this point Lara got up. 'I could really go for a glass of port right now,' she told our kids. 'To your dad's memory.'

They just kept on going, and I started laughing, and it just seemed to get funnier and funnier. Then, all of a sudden, it went from funny to incredibly precious. I began thinking what a beautiful moment it was. While still alive, I got to experience how my family was going to act and react and talk to each other when I'm gone. And it was so cool. As I was sitting there, I started to pretend like I really *was* dead. So I wasn't going to talk, or interrupt; I'd just watch the show.

My daughter said, 'He was such a good guy.'

'Yeah,' my son said, 'but he could be a prick sometimes.'

'He sure could,' Lara agreed, 'but I'm glad you guys are here with me.'

I was so grateful and appreciative because I now knew that

when I go, they'll live on. They can move on. And I know exactly what they're going to be doing to remember me. And that they *will* remember me. The good, bad, funny and sad. It told me I can let it go and not have to worry about it. I can be prepared for death.

Because that's what it's all about, isn't it? There are a million ways to live, but the only inevitability is death. A very funny man once said the only sure things in life are death and taxes. He was only half right. If you've got the right accountant, you can get away without paying what you owe for decades. Ask any billionaire. Or the church. But death. That's the great equaliser. The ultimate democracy. It's coming for you and me and all of us, whether we like it or not.

So I'm prepared for that. There'll be no bad feelings anymore. There'll be no more sorrow. No more pain. Well, there might be some pain, but not like there would have been if I weren't prepared. I've known doctors and others who work with people at the end of life, and they're the same. They're prepared for death. They've lived with it so long the mystery is gone, and so is the fear. It's just the end of the journey, that's all.

I've had the most amazing few years since I crashed my first funeral. I know the rest of the world fell apart during COVID-19, and a lot of people had a really shit time, but I went the other way. It's like Lara always says, I'm always heading in the opposite direction to everyone else.

Being so close to so much death, and spending time with people as they tie up their loose ends, has opened my eyes and given me a new and much better perspective. Not only am I prepared to die, but I'm also prepared to lose someone really close to me. Once you accept that, you can live without worry. I used to worry all the time. But I'm mentally ready. Losing a loved one won't be a shock. It won't be traumatising. Sure, it'll be painful. But at the same time, I'll be empowered to move on.

I'm braced for the end. If you're not braced, if you're not expecting death, if you have to process everything in the moment, it can be shattering. You can't be your best self, and the best help to your loved ones. If you're panicking in the moment, you risk breaking when you have to be strong.

* * *

Before I shut down Coffin Camping, I decided to spend a night in a box. Not for any other reason than just because. I wanted to experience what it was like to lie in a coffin not for a few minutes but for a whole night. With the lid shut. This is something that'd terrify many people, and I was nervous, sure, but I had my mobile phone, which gave me light and the comfort of knowing that if I got stuck inside I could make a call. So I shut myself in, lay back, and let my mind wander into the darkest of places. At a certain point, I decided to try to speak to the dead. I spoke to my best friend Michael who died when we were very young, my uncle-in-law who recently died, who I missed, and a woman who I wished was my own mother and also missed. None of them spoke back to me but I did enjoy the experience. It was quite cathartic letting them know what I'd been up to over the years.

I talked about my life and where I was now and asked if they could send me a sign that might make me believe they could hear me. No sign came from beyond, but it was nice to reflect on and talk to all the people I had met who were now dead. It was also nice to tell them how much I missed them. They left me feeling humbled, blessed, content and happy to be alive.

Death can come without warning, leaving you with no time to say goodbye to those you love and no time to get your affairs in order. As I lay in that closed casket, I thought about all the things I would do if I knew when I was going to die. I thought about spending my last day with those I loved, and spending the night making love to the one I love most of all. And of course I thought about taking out a large loan from some cunt banker and blowing it all on one massive party. Why not make the most of this life? Whether there is a heaven or a hell we must do our best to be our best and accept death as a part of life.

One of my clients was terrified of dying. He didn't want to go, and to be honest the thought of it probably contributed to him dying. How's that for fucking irony. Most people I meet have already accepted it; some hope it comes quickly, others don't give it a second thought. I think about it every day and was doing so long before I became the Coffin Confessor. It kept me alive. It also gave me the ability to live without worrying about it. I accepted it into my life just as I accepted many other things, such as pain, suffering, joy and love.

Still lying in the casket asking for a sign from the beyond, I heard something. A strange, faraway drone. I listened intently, until I realised it was the unmistakable sound of a car pulling up to the gate of my property. I then heard someone yelling, 'Bury me in satin, Coffin Confessor!' It was at that moment I knew

Coffin Camping was a goner, so I said goodnight to the dead, and told them I'd see them when I saw them, and climbed out of the box.

* * *

Lara and I have been together for nearly forty years. If we're lucky, we've got another good twenty or thirty years together. But eventually one of us is going to die. I know it's going to happen. I see us lying together in a bed, but I don't see what happens next. Do we go together? Do I just let her go? Lara says she wouldn't want to live without me, but I tell her that's crazy. Even though I'll be dead, I'll be alive as long as she remembers me.

Life is quick. One moment you're here, the next you're not, and, for a lot of people, some relative you hardly know is sorting through your shit deciding what goes to charity and what might fetch a buck on Gumtree. That's going to happen to the Blakes of the world. But it's not going to happen to me. Because I'll be remembered. By Lara, by my kids, by my grandkids. I want them to remember me as I am now, not as I was without them. Because when I didn't have them, I was going through shit. They got all the closure. I want them to remember me as the funniest, most loving and most beautiful person on the planet. Someone they couldn't live without. Even though they will inevitably have to.

But I'll always be there in their memories.

And if their memories fail them, they can just google me. Which is cool – I like that aspect of fame. After I'm gone, if they want to see me or hear my voice, they can find me on the internet.

They can spend time with me that way. In their memories and on the internet, I'll always be here, telling the world to sit down, shut up, or fuck off, because the guy in the coffin still has something to say.

Acknowledgements

My life-light began to flicker until your presence had me shine brighter than the sun. To my grandchildren Bear, Cooper, Luna, Archie, Ollie and Aura. May you all live a full, loving and adventurous life. Never let fear hold you back.

No regrets,

Love Popeye.

ALSO BY BILL EDGAR

'A fascinating and thought-provoking read.' GOOD READING

BILL EDGAR
THE COFFIN CONFESSOR

ONE MAN'S FIGHT TO SURVIVE THE PAST AND LEAVE NOTHING TO FATE

1

It's your funeral

It was a perfect day for a funeral. A bright summer morning on the Gold Coast. In a few hours the heat and humidity would skyrocket, baking the steepled roof until the chapel was oven hot. But for now the weather was on the side of the mourners, who shuffled into the church to pay their respects to the deceased. The men wore simple black suits, the women tasteful knee-length dresses in muted tones, with the occasional splash of colour.

I filed in along with them, sombre, head bowed respectfully while we took our seats, chairs scraping and shoes squeaking.

The ceremony opened with a few words from the priest, a hymn, and then a big fellow seated in the pews stood up and slowly made his way to the lectern. There, he stood for a moment, shuffling the papers he'd prepared for the eulogy. He introduced himself as John, the best friend of Graham, the deceased, and welcomed us to his farewell. They'd all known and loved Graham, and they'd all miss him.

John was a big guy – the silver-haired, red-faced Queensland farmer type used to getting his own way. The sort of man who wore a big, easy smile on his face as he made his way through the world. But his mouth turned down as he cast a sad look towards the coffin that held his best friend in the whole world, Graham Anderson.

John stared off into the chapel mournfully, took a deep breath, then began to speak. The crowd listened respectfully as he delivered his opening words. His voice echoed through the chapel, over the sound of gentle weeping from some of the mourners. It was a beautiful scene, a Hollywood-perfect opening to a funeral service.

After exactly two minutes had passed, as arranged, I stood, tugged my suit vest down to neaten it, and cleared my throat. I reached into my vest pocket to retrieve a letter.

'Excuse me, but I'm going to need you to sit down, shut up, or fuck off. The man in the box has a few things to say.'

Every eye in the room turned to me. The priest's jaw hit the floor. He didn't know what was happening – he was in shock, by the looks of things. But my attention was focused on John. He was the one I had come to confront, and I kept an eye on the would-be eulogist while reading from the letter, which Graham had given me.

By the way the colour drained from John's face, I could tell he knew what this was about. He was shit-scared. As well he should have been.

I'll explain why in a moment, but first we'll have to go back in time a few months, back to when I first met Graham, the man lying in the coffin. He'd hired me as a private investigator.

* * *

It's your funeral

Being a private investigator – or PI if you're short on time – is pretty much what it says on the tin: my clients hire me to investigate things that someone else would prefer to remain private. If you believe the way we're portrayed in the books, films and the media, you'd think most of that work is following cheating spouses around with a telephoto lens camera. And you'd be right.

A huge percentage of PI work is just men and women who have grown suspicious of their significant other and want someone to bring them evidence that confirms that suspicion. There are whole agencies dedicated to this line of work. They'll hang around and stalk your spouse until they can bring you the unhappy proof that they are running around on you.

That was never my forte, nor was it something I particularly enjoyed doing. The way I see it, if you're so suspicious of your partner that you're prepared to hire a PI, then I can guarantee your marriage has problems. I'll save you some cash by telling you what you already know: they're screwing around, and you'd be better off hiring a marriage counsellor than a PI.

Apart from infidelity, nearly every other job involves looking into some kind of commercial problem for the client. Theft, fraud, blackmail. In the end, most PI work comes down to money. Love and money – the only two things that get your average person worked up enough to call a PI.

Graham's case involved a little of both. He first engaged me in early 2016 to investigate his finances. A farmer in his mid-sixties, Graham was a self-made man. But he'd recently fallen ill, and had been unable to keep up with the workload of managing his business. He had a suspicion that, while he was laid low, his accountant was taking advantage of his reduced faculties. He'd noticed a little money going missing here and there, and things weren't quite adding up; he had a gut feeling that someone was ripping him off.

Graham reached out to me because I have certain skills in that area, but I couldn't take the job straight away because I was flat out with other work. But Graham wanted my skill-set in particular, and he was happy to wait.

When I was finally available to investigate properly, about half a year later, I worked out what was going on fairly quickly. Money *was* being funnelled from his accounts, and I was able to figure out by whom. With enough pressure applied to the accountants in question, the money was returned and the case was closed. Graham considered it a good result.

Sadly, that's where the good news ended for Graham. He was in worse health than he'd let on, and at the conclusion of my investigation, as we were wrapping up, he disclosed that he was terminally ill. He'd been happy to wait the six months it took for me to take the case on because he thought he had plenty of time. That turned out not to be the case.

'I thought I had longer than this,' he told me, as I sat by the bed he could no longer leave. 'But I suppose everyone thinks that. You get told you've got just a few months to live and you think, *Oh yeah, whatever, I feel great, I'm going to live for years*. I didn't know it was all going to go this fast.'

Our conversation led to matters of mortality – death, the afterlife. Graham wasn't really afraid of dying, but he was curious about what happens to us after we close our eyes that final time.

'I don't have any idea what'll go on after I'm gone, or where I'm going to end up, but wouldn't it be nice to know?'

'Well, let me know once you find out,' I said. 'Send some sign from the other side. Let me know if you enjoyed your funeral.'

He shook his head. 'I don't reckon I will. I already know I'm going to hate my funeral.'

Graham told me that he didn't think much of most of the funerals he'd been to. He was always surprised and disappointed, because he'd expect to see a true reflection of his loved one in the memorial service – the things that made them unique, that people loved them for. The good *and* the bad. Instead, he got a sanitised, watered-down picture of some kind of saint, delivered by a priest that nine out of ten times didn't know the deceased from a bar of soap. He'd even had friends who had recorded their own video eulogies, only for their message to be considered inappropriate for some reason, and the service instead ran a slideshow of photos from their life.

Graham mentioned that he'd like to write his own eulogy. He'd fill it with the things that really mattered to him, leaving the world in a way that he felt actually represented the way he'd lived.

'Why don't you do that?' I said. 'Film a video and get them to run it at the service.'

'I know they would never run it. Someone would decide it was too confronting for my family and friends, and they'd be afraid of insulting those left behind. There's no point.'

'I could always do it for you,' I joked. 'Crash your funeral and deliver the eulogy that you really want.'

We had a laugh about it, shook hands, and said goodbye. I didn't give it another thought.

But a few weeks later I received a call from Graham.

'I've been thinking,' he said down the line. 'I'm going to take you up on that offer.'

'What offer?'

'I want you to crash my funeral. Interrupt the service and read out the message I'm going to write for you.'

'Are you serious?'

'Dead serious. And I'm going to pay you ten grand to do it.'

Fuck me, I thought. 'That's a lot of money.'

'There's a lot I want to say. You see, there's something I want revealed at my funeral. My best mate, John, is insisting on giving the eulogy.'

'So? What's wrong with that?'

'He's also trying to screw my wife.'